THE MICROSCOPE MADE EASY

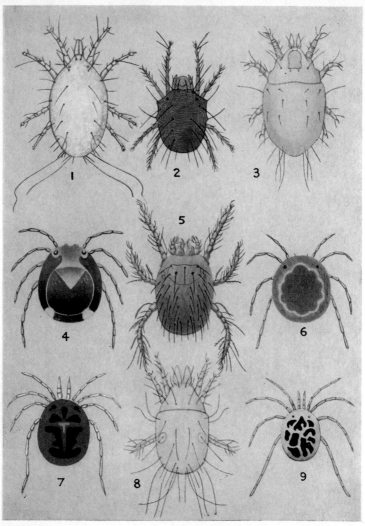

Plate I

Mites

Frontispiece

1. *Carpoglyphus lactis.* Sugar Mite. Female. 0.45mm.
2. *Metalebranychus ulmi.* Fruit Tree Red Spider. Female. 0.4mm.
3. *Rhizoglyphus echinopus.* Narcissus Bulb Mite. Male. 0.7mm.
4. *Arrhenurus caudatus.* Water Mite. Female. 1.2mm.
5. *Trombicula autumnalis.* Larva. Harvest Mite. 0.22mm.
6. *Diplodontus despiciens.* Water Mite. Female. 2mm.
7. *Limnesia fulgida.* Male. 1.8mm.
8. *Tyrolichus casei.* Cheese Mite. 1mm.
9. *Hygrobates longipalpis.* Water Mite. 2.5mm.

THE MICROSCOPE
MADE EASY

By

A. LAURENCE WELLS

Author of
Tropical Aquariums, Plants and Fishes
Garden Ponds, Fish and Fountains etc.

With fifteen Plates and
twenty-six Line Illustrations

FREDERICK WARNE & CO., LTD.
LONDON AND NEW YORK

Printed in Great Britain

CONTENTS

LIST OF ILLUSTRATIONS

CHAPTER I

INTRODUCTION TO MICROSCOPY

THE would-be microscopist is often baffled, bewildered and usually made thoroughly disheartened by his first attempts at viewing objects under his microscope. This state of mind is further accentuated, as a general rule, when a textbook on mounting objects for the microscope is consulted.

The purpose of this book is to show that a very great many simple, though extremely interesting, objects can be mounted—that is to say, so prepared that they may be seen at their best when highly magnified—easily and inexpensively.

Usually, one's first microscope has come as a present from a friend or relative or has been purchased second-hand because it was cheap; or, maybe, it was bought with the laudable object of emulating Dr. John Thorndyke or another of the scientific detectives. On the other hand the instrument may have been obtained so that the many beautiful and interesting creatures of minute form that inhabit sea, pond, garden or wayside could be observed and studied. Perhaps the idea was to examine dust or the variety of structure to be found in textiles or to see the construction of hairs, rocks, crystals—oh! hundreds and hundreds of wonderful things.

Then came bitter disillusion; the objects, no matter how one tried or how one manipulated the microscope, looked shapeless, colourless lumps, without design or form.

Somehow it seems to the novice that slide-making is a mystic sort of business and that there must be some magic touchstone necessary before success crowns one's messy efforts. The more textbooks that are consulted the stronger becomes the suspicion that this 'touchstone' consists of a great quantity of expensive chemicals and apparatus that only a Rockefeller could buy or a Doctor of Science use. As a result the microscope is put away regretfully and forgotten and microscopy is put down as being an overrated pastime.

The information given in most textbooks on microscope technique is sound and of great value, provided the reader has a thorough knowledge of chemistry, optics—and microscopy. The tyro cannot see the wood for the trees, his perspective is lost in a welter of alternative techniques and long, complicated formulae.

The whole basic principle of preparing and

mounting objects to be seen under the microscope may be summed up in a Euclidian Theorem, viz. :

'It is required that the object is to be so prepared and mounted that, so far as is possible, the structure can be seen clearly and without distortion even under high powers.

It is further required that the object should be so mounted that, also so far as is possible, it will retain its colour, shape and form for an indefinite period. Q.E.F.'

The above remarks should be borne in mind all the time. It does not matter how an object is mounted or in what medium, so long as those are observed—I have even heard of a man who used golden syrup as a mountant for daphnia and other small creatures. True, there are a number of objects that require rather lengthy and complicated processes before their essential parts are revealed; in the ordinary way microscopy of this nature is beyond the interests of the man in the street. That is, unless his inclinations lead him to specialize in one field or another and in that case, by the time he has advanced so far, the textbook will be of great help. Indeed, when he has grasped the basic principles, he will be evolving intricate methods of his own to assist in solving his own particular problems.

Certain objects, however, refuse to submit to simple methods and some of these make interesting preparations and are of especial value in 'showing off' what the microscope will do, for the benefit of friends. Some of these preparations are given towards the end of this book. In fact, the most simple mounting methods are given first, followed by the other methods in the order of their difficulty.

If a microscope has been given to us we may say 'Thank you very much', of course, and, if it is an inferior instrument, make the best of it. If, on the other hand, money is no object then all that has to be done is to consult a reputable maker who will advise the best instrument for one's particular purpose.

When there is but little money available then a good second-hand instrument is indicated, but, in buying second-hand microscopes, as in buying other things, there are pitfalls. What must be looked for in a good microscope, then? First of all, do not be dazzled by a great array of accessories, these are very often quite useless and are no indication of the quality of the instrument. See rather that the base is firm and substantial, not easily knocked over or affected by vibrations; look to all movable parts and see that there is a smooth action, not stiff nor yet too free so that there is a wobble. This is most important in the racking arrangement of the tube itself; if the racking gear is worn and loose the slightest movement will cause a tremor that may have the appearance of a minor earthquake when high powers are being used.

The mirror, too, should have a smooth action. If its pivots are too stiff the object may be disarranged in your efforts to manipulate it. On the other hand, if it is loose you may find that, after you have adjusted it to your satisfaction, it will creep into some other position of its own choosing.

A sub-stage is a great asset, high powers will derive considerable assistance from a condenser and crystals will look even more beautiful with a polarizer. Both of these pieces of apparatus require a sub-stage to hold them. The action of the sub-stage, as with the other adjustable parts, should be smooth.

A triple nose-piece, although not a necessity, is a great convenience. This screws into the tube where the object glass is ordinarily screwed and has three holes, with screw threads, each taking an objective. By turning it round each lens in turn is brought into use, thus providing various magnifications without having to remove the lenses.

So much for the stand—I have omitted men-

PLATE II
FRESHWATER AND MARINE ALGAE.

1. *Nostoc Linchia.* Occurs as greenish-blue bead-like strands of a gelatinous nature sticking to mosses or floating on the surface.

2. *Zygnogonum ericetorum.* A very common and widely distributed filamentous alga which has adapted itself to a terrestrial mode of life. In shady situations the filaments are green but when exposed to the sun they turn purple.

3. Spermatozoids. These are the male reproductive elements in algae. They are formed as swarmers in special cells and when released swim about until they encounter the female element, usually contained within an oogonium, the counterpart of the ovary in a flowering plant.

4. *Ulothrix zonata.* Common in flowing water where it forms bright green patches, particularly in spring and autumn.

5. *Zygnema stellinum* (conjugating). In this species of freshwater alga the filament of female cells (on the left) differs considerably from the filament of male cells. At the stage here illustrated conjugation is completed.

6. *Spirogyra zygospore.* The resultant 'egg' from the conjugation of two cells.

7. *Eudorina elegans.* Sometimes this beautiful alga is so very prolific in small ponds in spring as to turn the water green in a few days. They are usually found in clusters of from 30-40 individuals.

8. *Botrydium granulatum.* The so-called 'Mud Alga'. It is found exclusively standing out in masses on drying mud at the sides of ponds and ditches, sometimes in vast numbers.

9. *Scenedesmus quadricauda.* A freshwater alga which forms colonies of from 4-8 individuals, sometimes 16. They are very small, the total length of the colony may not exceed 1/300".

10. *Tribonema bombycinum.* A freshwater filamentous alga which is sometimes found covered with patches of a yellow-brown ferric carbonate mucus, due to the iron-bacteria which live within it.

11. *Chroococcopsis gigantea.* A unicellular member of the blue-green algae group.

12. *Callithamnion corymbosum.* The illustration is of a small fragment of an inch high tufted seaweed which grows on submerged rocks in temperate seas. The deeper coloured ovals are tetraspores, the reproductive bodies.

13. *Fucus vesiculosus* (mature oogonium). The female reproductive body of the familiar Bladder wrack of the seashore.

14. *Corallina officinalis.* This illustrates a minute portion of the calcareous seaweed which is found on stones and shells between tide marks in the northern hemisphere and which looks like a microscopic fir tree.

15. *Polysiphonia apaca.* Like the foregoing, the complete plant, of which this is a microscopic portion, resembles a tiny tree. It is also of similar habitat.

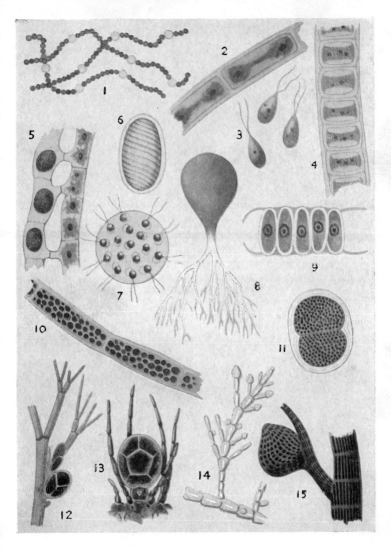

Plate II

Plate III

PLATE III

SINGLE-CELLED ALGAE AND ANIMAL FORMS

1. *Ceratium hirundinella*. A freshwater dinoflagellate. Note the median groove in which the flagella lie when the organism is at rest. Colour greenish. Length 1/280" to 1/140".

2. *Hydrodictyon reticulatum*. The Water Net, a rather rare alga which sometimes occurs in prodigious quantities. The hollow, cylindrical network may reach a diameter of nine inches.

3. *Draparnaldia glomerata*. A filamentous freshwater alga which consists of a main filament which bears tufts of smaller filaments, usually embedded in a thin envelope of mucilage.

4. *Volvox globator*. A single-celled alga frequently found in shallow pools in spring and summer. The largest specimens have a diameter of up to 1/30".

5. *Spirogyra majuscula*. This is one of a large family of filamentous algae, the various members of which are usually to be found in small pieces of stagnant water. They are easily recognizable by the spiral bands of the chloroplast.

6. *Paramoecium*. This is a single-celled animal although it is of a green colour, due to minute algae living within the cell wall. It is common in stagnant water.

7. *Peridinium cinctum*. One of the armoured dinoflagellates. The armour in some species is silicified. Some species are marine but this is a freshwater species and is found amongst *Confervae*.

8. *Chaetophora incrassata*. Closely related to *Draparnaldia*, but without the main filament. Is found in small green patches (a portion of which is here illustrated) in fresh water.

9. *Pleurococcus (Protococcus) vulgaris*. A unicellular terrestrial alga found in damp places, usually on the windward side of tree trunks, walls, palings, etc.

10. *Noctiluca miliaris (scintillans)*. A cystoflagellate found abundantly in the sea and even in estuaries. It is a leaf-like organism and is highly phosphorescent.

11. *Pediastrum boryanum*. Common in ponds and ditches amongst the water plants. Usually found in disc-shaped colonies of up to 128 extremely minute cells.

tion of many parts connected with it and referred only to the essentials—and now for the lenses; they are the life-blood, as you might say, of the whole instrument. You may have the most mag-

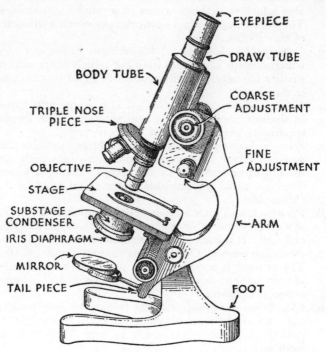

FIG. I.—MICROSCOPE WITH TRIPLE NOSE-PIECE

nificent stand that ever instrument maker contrived, yet, with poor lenses, you are in a worse plight than the man with an antique instrument that has good lenses.

If there are already lenses of an inferior quality with the instrument, then there is nothing to do but make the best of them, but at the first opportunity purchase a good lens from a reliable firm; and in this respect it is well worth noting that one really good lens is of greater service than a host of inferior ones. Some people collect lenses as others collect foreign stamps; they spend their time trying one or other of them, litter their table with a host of objectives and eye-pieces of a variety of powers, and, in the end, achieve nothing. Quality and not quantity applies more forcibly here than anywhere else.

Two kinds of lenses are required before a properly magnified view is obtained. First we must have an *ocular*, otherwise known as an *eye-piece*. This is inserted in the tube at the end where the eye is applied. Two sizes are used according to the design of the instrument, the usual size having an outside diameter of 23.2 mm. and being known as the student size as shown in Fig. 1; the other size, known as 'capped', has an outside diameter of 32.26 mm. and can only be used with a certain type of instrument.

They are obtainable in various powers which seem to vary according to the maker, a rather foolish state of affairs and one that is likely to mislead the student. The No. 1 of one maker may

17

have a magnification of 3 diameters or less, and the same number of another may magnify to 5, or more, diameters. However, a low and a high power should be obtained if at all possible.

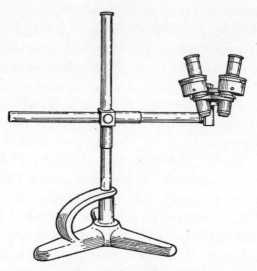

FIG. 2.—LOW-POWER BINOCULAR MICROSCOPE FOR VIEWING OBJECTS STEREOSCOPICALLY. IT HAS A LONG WORKING DISTANCE

The second type of lens is known as the objective, or the object-glass. The objective is found at the lower end of the microscope tube, facing the object to be examined. It is held in position by a universal screw-thread to allow objectives to be interchanged at will. Each objective, according to its kind, magnifies a certain number of diameters; the various 'powers', as these degrees of magnification are called, are not designated by numbers as are the eye-pieces. Instead, they are based on a rather complicated formula, the details of which are beyond my ability to put simply in a few words. Suffice it to say, then, that these formulae resolve themselves into a measurement of length. Most things about the microscope are topsy-turvy, so it is not surprising to discover that the 'length' of a high power is considerably less than that of a low one. Thus the objective known as the '3-inch' is one of the very lowest powers and that known as the '$\frac{1}{12}$-inch' is a very high power indeed. When in focus the latter lens nearly touches the slide, in fact oil or water must fill the space between the lens and slide. In using them a drop of cedar-wood oil is placed on the slide, and the tube racked down until the lens touches the oil, then focused; that is, if it is an 'oil immersion' lens. The other kind, requiring water instead of oil, is known as a 'water immersion' lens.

As the lenses decrease in power so the distance between them and the slide increases, until, with the 3-inch objective it is about two inches away when in focus.

Naturally, there are objectives and objectives,

and it can be accepted as an unassailable fact that a good $\frac{2}{3}$-in. lens with a correspondingly good eye-piece will reveal more than an indifferent $\frac{1}{6}$-in. Magnification alone is not everything, there must be sharp-cut definition (meaning clarity of outline, etc.) as well and this can be obtained only by using good lenses and by accurate adjustment, not only of the focal length but of the mirror too. A sub-stage condenser, usually adjustable, also helps. Most microscopes are so constructed that the distance between the eye-piece and the objective can be altered, like the length of a telescope, by pulling out the inner-tube (draw-tube) slightly. The greater the distance between the two lenses the larger the field will be and consequently there will be greater magnification. In the more elaborate instrument, such as is used for very fine and accurate work, the draw-tube is adjusted by means of a rack and pinion.

The most usual lenses contained in a complete equipment are $\frac{2}{3}$-in., $\frac{1}{3}$-in. and $\frac{1}{6}$-in. objectives and a low and a high power eye-piece. Thus, with the $\frac{2}{3}$-in. objective in conjunction with the low-power eye-piece to the $\frac{1}{6}$-in. objective with the high-power eye-piece you will have a range of from about 50 magnification to 600. The principal advantage of having a high-power eye-piece is that extra magnification can be obtained without disturbing the focus unduly.

Before leaving the microscope itself, just a word on maintenance. Treat the microscope well and it will give good and efficient service for several lifetimes; there is many an old instrument that has been cared for properly that is capable of better service than a neglected modern one. To clean up an old dilapidated instrument rub the brass-work over with a soft rag soaked in a mixture of equal parts of olive oil and turpentine. Remove as much of the oil as you can with a clean rag; this will, in any case, leave a very thin film which will help to prevent verdigris from forming on the brass parts or rust on the iron. Do not use metal or any other polish, whether liquid or powder, the mixture mentioned will do all that is necessary without injuring the lacquer.

Besides corrosion, the mechanical parts will be rendered less efficient by dust. Here, as in slide-making, dust is the arch-enemy. It is obvious that after use the microscope and all the extra equipment should be put away in a case, yet many a microscopist is inclined to neglect this, promising himself that he will put it away after tea or supper, or something like that. The result is that the instrument may be left out all night and in the morning may have a film of dust, or, worse still, of moisture covering the whole. Also, if the instrument is being used for a protracted period—whilst slide-making, for instance—fine dust, insidious and almost imperceptible, will get into the working parts. An old glass bell-jar, or a modern plastic cover, of sufficient size to cover completely the whole instrument is of great value; it can be removed or replaced in a second. An inexpensive and satisfactory substitute can be made from sheets of cellophane which may be bought at most stationers. Cut a number of triangular strips, the length depending on the height of the instrument, and stick them together, edge to edge. The number of strips will vary according to the bulk of the microscope; for the ordinary type about nine strips will be required, having a base measurement of six inches and a total length of eighteen inches or slightly less.

After use the lenses should be put away in their respective boxes. Use an old silk handkerchief to clean the lens itself; failing this, an old and soft linen cloth will do, but this is apt to leave small wisps of cotton behind. A very soft, thin paper known as Japanese rice paper is sold for the express purpose of cleaning lenses but this, too, is inclined to leave tiny filaments behind. Ordinary tissue paper does not clean efficiently; when all is said and done a piece of silk is the best.

There are two more small items, small enough in themselves it is true, but of importance in the long run. The first is to do with the stage; when examining objects in the live box or in liquid on the slide a certain amount of moisture may spill over; be sure to wipe this up at once for, not only may it encourage rust, it is difficult to manipulate a slide on a wet stage. The other point also concerns moisture, this time from the condensation of breath particularly just below the eye-piece. The beadlets of moisture so formed may be overlooked but unless wiped off before the instrument is put away will eventually give an air of neglect to what is, after all, a most delicate piece of apparatus.

Finally, and this applies more forcibly, perhaps, to old instruments, do not attempt to clean the inside of the lenses unless they can be got at without unscrewing the parts. Take them to an optician; he is familiar with the arrangement of lenses of all kinds, and for a very small fee he will clean them properly.

Now as regards the manipulation of the instrument: stand it on a firm table facing the light, whether a window if it is daytime or the gas or electric light if night. Incline the stand so that the eye can be applied comfortably to the eye-piece whilst you are sitting down. Some microscopes are not inclinable but as these are generally small they can be used quite easily without being inclined. Insert a low-power eye-piece in the top of the tube and fix your lowest power objective into its respective place. If it is, say a $\frac{2}{3}$-in. objective, rack down so that it is about half an inch from the stage. Now manipulate the mirror and endeavour to throw a beam of light on to the objective; you may have to tilt it away from you a little or towards you, or from side to side. Practise throwing the mirror out of the light and bringing the beam back again from various directions until it is only a matter of seconds to put it right. The most comfortable way of manipulating the mirror is to rest both forearms on the table and use two hands in the adjustment.

With most microscopes there is included in the outfit a test slide, maybe of diatoms, maybe of the common flea which, for some unknown reason, is popular among microscopists, as a mounted object, I mean. Place the slide on the stage and fix firmly in place with the two clips provided for the purpose; the student who can run to a mechanical stage will not require clips, instead the slide will be kept in place by two metal strips which grip the top and bottom edges of the slide.

Look down the microscope and adjust the

mirror. At first you may see nothing but a blurred shadow; rack the tube down by turning the milled-heads of the coarse adjustment away from you. Do this slowly or else there may be disaster through the lens crashing through the cover-glass to the complete annihilation of the slide and the possible scratching of the lens.

Gradually the object will take a more or less definite shape. Rack gently back and forth, a tiny movement each way, until you reach the clearest focus. Now turn the milled-head of the fine adjustment a little, now this way, now that, until the clearest image possible is obtained. The result may not be all that you had hoped for; details may be entirely obliterated by the brilliant light from the mirror; possibly the window, if that is the source of light, will be superimposed in miniature over the object in such a way as to spoil the view. The latter annoyance will disappear if the microscope is moved to a different part of the room, nearer the window for preference.

And now for the excess of light from the mirror; nearly all microscopes made within the past eighty years, other than the small, rigid kind, have a diaphragm of sorts fitted to the underside of the stage. The best type is the 'Iris' diaphragm made of a number of black-painted discs which can be made to converge until a bare pin-point of light is allowed through the objective—the diaphragm of a camera has a similar action and a similar use, i.e. that of controlling the amount of light on the lens.

Many instruments have a different type of diaphragm and this consists of a circular piece of blackened metal with a number of holes drilled around the edge; these, starting with a very tiny hole about a sixteenth of an inch in diameter, increase gradually in size to the largest hole, about five-eighths of an inch in diameter. This disc is set slightly to one side of the underpart of the stage, so that, when it is rotated, each hole in turn occupies the centre of the aperture in the stage itself.

Adjust the diaphragm until the delicate parts of the object reveal themselves, but not so as to darken the rest of the field. If there is a kind of glare about the field cut a disc of ordinary white paper the size of the mirror and place this over the mirror. On the other hand, if there is no diaphragm at all, and you do not feel equal to making a simple one, place one or more fingers of the right hand over the mirror and so cut out some of the light. Conversely, tilt the mirror slightly out of true so that the full beam is not thrown on the lens. These, however, are but subterfuges and do not produce the clear-cut definition one hopes for.

There are one or two other slight adjustments that, in their small way, add to the clarity of the magnified object. By slightly lengthening the draw-tube, as explained earlier, the field is enlarged and this may or may not effect an improvement. Again, if one is lucky enough to have a condenser (known as 'sub-stage condenser') fitted below the stage, the light from the mirror can be 'focused' on the object. Such a condenser is of great value when using the $\frac{1}{6}$-in. objective or those of shorter focus. Generally speaking, the shorter the focus of the lens the nearer the condenser must be to the object, but do not rack it up so close that the diaphragm will not work.

The image will also be rendered less distinct if light is allowed to fall directly on the top of the object. To obviate this have the instrument facing the source of light and so inclined that the top of the stage is in shadow; if, however, it is not possible to incline the stage (you must keep it level, for instance, if examining a drop of water) make a screen of paper which can either be clipped to the stage or have the bottom edge resting on the stage and the top against the tube. Top light, as will be explained later on, is of great value for certain purposes, but when bottom light alone is required it is a nuisance.

Now, with both forearms resting on the table—the fingers will not tremble so much this way—move the slide by holding it 'gently but firmly' with the thumb and forefinger of each hand. Owing to the image being inverted you must move the slide from left to right if you want to move the image from right to left; this applies to the up-and-down movement also. With practice one becomes quite used to this topsy-turvy business.

Having explored all the possibilities of the slide remove the eye-piece and insert the high-power one; little, if any, additional focusing will be required. The difference between the two lenses will be noticeable, less of the object will appear within the field and details hitherto obscure will reveal themselves. Incidentally, if there are dust spots in the view remove the slide and clean it back and front with a piece of silk or soft cloth; if they persist slowly turn the eye-piece. If the spots are caused by dust on the eye-piece they will move as it is turned. Failing this, and if they remain more or less in focus when the tube is racked up or down, clean the objective. They may be actually within the slide itself through the dust settling whilst it was being made; such dust is fairly obvious as belonging to the slide. The spots may still remain, in spite of the mirror being dust-free, and in that case it is the inside of the lenses that are dirty—this state of affairs very rarely occurs with a new instrument but is quite common with very old ones—and so, as already advised, the services of an optician should be sought.

Now remove the objective and replace it with the next power which, in the majority of cases, will be the $\frac{1}{3}$-in. Rack the tube up before unscrewing the objective—there is barely room for this when it is in focus—and replace the lens in its respective case, lest you knock it off the table. In focusing the $\frac{1}{3}$-in., the lens is brought to about a quarter of an inch from the slide. Change the eye-piece and replace it with the low-power; the reason for this is, that at this initial stage we must get a relative idea of the value of each combination of lenses and the best way we can do that is by working upwards, one power at a time. Moreover, the temptation to try a number of different slides should be avoided; ring the changes on the other slides after the mind's eye has grasped how one particular object responds to different magnifications.

With each increase in power the lens has to be closer to the slide and so more care than ever is required in focusing, especially with the coarse adjustment. Slight alterations may have to be made to the length of the draw-tube (though for general purposes this does not matter very much) and the condenser may have to be brought nearer the stage. The diaphragm may, and probably will, have to be opened to admit more light.

Still continue to roam over the subject of the slide. You will find that the slightest movement now has a violent effect but you will also find that your hands are getting accustomed to their task.

And now for the $\frac{1}{6}$-in. objective; a valuable lens this, when once it has been mastered, but quite useless otherwise. When in focus it is a bare eighth of an inch from the slide so regard it from the side as the tube is racked down, so that the distance can be judged (this lens is the champion slide smasher). Stop racking at about an eighth of an inch from the slide and continue the process of focusing with the fine adjustment. Plenty of light will be required and so the diaphragm may have to be opened to its fullest. Use the lower power eye-piece first and set out on an expedition over the vast tract of country that this highly magnified flea offers. After a while a slight jolt from the hand may send it out of the field altogether and there may be great difficulty in finding it again. The quickest way of doing this without altering the focus is to close the diaphragm until only a pin-point of light shines on the slide; now move the slide until the flea, if such it is that we are examining, is bathed in light and it will be found to be within the field again. The high-power eye-piece is now inserted and all the small adjustments hitherto mentioned carried out carefully and minutely. The hands that move the slide will be found to tremble violently, a bus or tram going by will set up distinct vibrations and anyone walking heavily over the floor will incur displeasure from the operator. This combination of lenses may have a magnification of 600 diameters or more. That is to say, they will give a postage stamp the area of an ordinary garden and a postcard that of a full-size football pitch.

Since the end of the war great strides have been made in almost every aspect of microscopy generally. Indeed, the enthusiast of a generation ago would certainly rub his eyes if he could see what is being done nowadays.

The usual types, of course, are still predominant but are more streamlined in design and of a less brassy finish—black enamel and chromium plate seems to be the most popular finish. In the really plutocratic models there may be two different types of interchangeable stages and interchangeable monocular and binocular bodies or drawtubes at a cost of upwards of £200. At the less plush end of the scale we find the humble 'student' model in a totally different guise from its counterpart of prewar years. Two such models are the Biolux (made by C. Baker of Holborn, Ltd.) and the Britex (made by Britex, Ltd.). In these the mirror has been dispensed with and instead there is built-in lighting so that the instrument may be used in any part of the room. Moreover, nothing can interfere with the lighting and so the focusing is done from the back of the instrument, a far more comfortable position for the operator. The cost, according to the lenses supplied, ranges from about £14 upwards and even at that price one may obtain a really workmanlike instrument capable of doing all that is required in a school laboratory, or, for example, ordinary plankton work. The lenses are the same as those used in the standard models.

I have referred to 'illumination' and the vagaries of ordinary daylight, particularly in respect of window reflection; to obviate these and to overcome the even greater vagaries of the usual forms of home lighting, a microscope lamp should be used. This consists, basically, of a stand into which a stout metal rod is fixed and to this rod a 'lamp-house' is attached in such a way that the lamp-house may be inclined at any desired angle. A lampholder such as is used for the ordinary kind of electric light bulb is fixed inside the 'house' and the whole is completed by a sufficient length of flex to reach the nearest electric point conveniently.

This, as I have said, is the basic principle, and, as such, should not be beyond the skill of the average handyman to make. From this simple design we progress to the elaborate types such as are used in photomicrography. These will have an iris diaphragm to adjust the light concentration and a filter holder, but this latter could well be made by the aforesaid handyman.

Light filters serve various purposes, according to their colour. Thus, if a specimen has been overstained, a filter of the appropriate colour will help to obviate this and, conversely, an understained specimen will be made more distinct by using the right filter. A pale blue or daylight-conversion filter will give the effect of daylight. On the other hand, if the microscope is to be used for long periods a yellow-green one will ease the strain on the eyes. If the illumination is too bright a neutral-grey filter can be used in addition to the coloured kind.

Many microscopists prefer built-in illumination

and it is the writer's opinion that this is the best method, other than when very high magnifications are being used or in photomicrography. Most of the best makers have produced attachments for this type of illumination. In principle, it consists of a small container in which a 6-watt bulb is housed together with a collector lens and diffuser. There is also an iris diaphragm and a filter holder. It is fixed under the sub-stage condenser in place of the mirror. The average price of this type of equipment is about £9 and this includes the necessary transformer and variable resistance.

CHAPTER II

HAVING mastered the manipulation of the instrument and having exhausted the possibilities of the slides, if any, that were included in the equipment, we look around for something else to examine. Near at hand are a multitude of extremely interesting objects, part of our everyday lives, that take on a very different aspect when highly magnified.

A cigarette picture, the ordinary coloured kind, not one of the glossy photographic variety, or a coloured picture from a book or magazine, makes an interesting subject. Clip it to the stage and so arrange the light, or move the position of the microscope, that the surface is illuminated; the mirror will not be used in this case. With a low-power objective we shall be able to see all that is required. The coloured part of the card will be seen to consist, not of smooth, unbroken colour, but of separate dots all the same distance apart on the white background. A piece of newsprint treated in the same way will be seen to have a very rough outline but the actual print is un-broken save where a fibre of the paper's com-position has refused to absorb the ink. This applies to handwriting also.

This brings us, of course, to paper itself, a sub-stance made in the first instance by macerating various materials, adding an adhesive—size or some similar matter—and putting the liquid through hot rollers. Esparto grass, a tall grass found commonly in Spain and North Africa, is used in the manufacture of particularly tough papers or mixed with other materials for writing paper. In fact, paper is almost entirely vegetable in composition; cotton, flax, hemp, straw, hops, jute, bamboo and other plants are used in the composition of various kinds of paper. Spruce, poplar and pine are ground up for the paper used for newsprint. Other vegetable matters are em-ployed also, including lalang, a broad-bladed grass grown in the Malay Peninsula, various barks and a number of coarse weeds that abound in tropical Australia. Consequently, it is some-thing of an adventure to examine paper under the microscope (the best quality writing papers, how-ever, are made from clean linen waste and so there is a lack of variety) and to pick out the various plants used.

The best results are obtained by soaking the

paper in water for twenty-four hours and then boiling it for a few minutes; the tissues can then be teased out easily with a mounted needle.

Plant fibres as well as the hairs of animals are dealt with more fully in a subsequent chapter; but plants also possess hairs of even a more varied nature than those of animals. With a sharp knife scrape up a piece of, say, wallflower leaf, grip the roughened tissues with a pair of tweezers (more correctly called forceps) and tear off a fragment of the thin cuticle. Place this on a slide; by folding it over the hairs on the edge may be seen in their entirety, otherwise a top view only is obtained. Use medium power lenses. In the case of the wallflower the hairs will be seen to be T-shaped just as the hairs of the chrysanthemum are. Southernwood, popularly known as 'old man', has T-shaped hairs also, but they are twisted like the horns of a ram. The dandelion has forked hairs whilst those of the hollyhock and lavender are star-like and branched. The petals of some plants, the snapdragon is one such, bear hairs too, and the stems of a great many plants also are hairy.

At the base of the hairs of the stinging-nettle are poison cells—when one touches these hairs they break off, being brittle, and the poison is liberated and enters the puncture so made.

An ordinary garden could keep the enthusiast occupied for months, even though plant hairs alone were studied; but the garden is a little world unto itself, each season brings its host of unseen creatures, eggs of insects, tiny insects themselves, rusts and moulds that attack fruit trees and other plants; if there happens to be a lily pond then yet another world is there to enlighten and interest the microscopist. In this short chapter on the things near at hand there is not room to enlarge on the things the garden has to offer. Nevertheless, we cannot dismiss it without making some reference to pollen. In the centre of nearly all flowers, on the stamens and pistils, is a yellowish powder. An outside agent—maybe bird, maybe insect—causes the pollen, formed within the anther of the stamen to be transferred to the sticky top of the pistil. A sugary sap causes the stickiness and in this sap the pollen proceeds to grow, breaking up into runners which form globules at their ends. These globules send out runners, too, and so the process goes on until the 'growth' has reached the seed capsule within the receptacle of the flower. The growth does not stop until it enters the seeds and so fertilizes them. Pollen can be made to perform for the benefit of the student in a simple manner. Make a mixture of sugar and water and smear a drop over a glass slip, then tap pollen from a flower on to the solution. In a short time the grains will be seen to send out arms and to grow as they do in the pistil of the plant. The pollen grains, themselves, display a great diversity of design, though nearly all have a roughened exterior; the reason for this, no doubt, is that they will not be shaken off easily once they have landed on the pistil.

Moss, likewise, is near at hand; in towns it may be found between paving stones in little frequented streets or between shaded brickwork or even in dried-up rain gutters, whilst in the country every sheltered bank has its cushions of velvety green. It makes a very pretty object under a fairly low-power; the 'leaves' should be separated, a drop of glycerine or liquid paraffin placed on them and covered with a cover-slip. Always a beautiful object, moss is even more beautiful and interesting when the spores are forming in spring and summer (see pages 165–6).

Let us now move from the garden to the larder and see what we can appropriate to further our insatiable quest for 'something to look at'.

Lift the lid of the cheese dish; if there is a piece of Stilton or Gorgonzola rind then it is practically certain that a yellowing brown dust has formed, generally where the rind has been resting. Put some of this dust on a glass slip and examine it with a medium-power. It will then resolve itself into a number of tiny mites, their hairy legs always on the move. These are the cheese mites, absolutely harmless; their chief function in life, apparently, is that of devouring the rind of ancient cheeses.

Should there be a fish in the larder remove several scales, put them in an egg-cup with some water and brush them with a camel- or sable-hair brush until all the mucus has been washed off. For a cursory examination place them on a slide, taking care to keep them separate and not over-lapping, and drain off all excess moisture with a piece of filter paper. Incidentally, the reason why filter paper is used to absorb moisture from a slide in preference to ordinary blotting paper is be-cause it will not leave pieces of fibre behind and so spoil the object. Place another slide on top and bind the two together with rubber bands at each end.

Use a low-power magnification and try both top light and transmitted light to see the different effects. If the scales are from a cod, hake, herring, whiting, sprat or similar fish, they will be roughly oval. Running parallel with the perimeter a num-ber of rings will be seen, some wider and more deeply indented than others; the deeper rings are the 'growth' rings and they indicate the winter seasons when the fish, in many species, ceases to feed or, in any case, to grow. Consequently, according to the number of these rings so the age of the fish may be told. The annual growth-rings of a tree are a parallel case.

An expert can trace the life history of the salmon from an examination of the scales, even to the number of times it has spawned and to how long it has spent in the sea and how long in fresh water. Also, from the scales of the herring, and other fishes, we can tell from the growth-rings the length of the fish at each year of its life, provided the length of the fish is known when it was captured.

The scales just described are known as 'cycloid' scales, but many fishes have a different kind, principally the flat-fishes; known as 'ctenoid' (meaning 'comb-like') they have a rectangular shape with one jagged edge. The age of the fish in this instance, too, can be ascertained from the growth rings. Incidentally, in recent years another mode of detecting the age of a fish has been evolved which has proved particularly effective with the cod. A portion of the dorsal fin is removed and cut through about half an inch from the body. The fin-ray is inserted in a piece of plasticine, to hold it firm, and the cut surface is examined with a low-power with plenty of top light. The yearly growth-rings can then be seen. In the Fisheries Laboratory at Lowestoft a tiny circular saw is used to make this cross-section; it does not distort the fin-ray so much as a razor or sharp knife would.

Nearly all fishes, whether with cycloid or ctenoid scales, have another kind of scale along the lateral line. This line runs from just behind the gills along the centre of the side to the base of the tail. In some fishes, the dab, for example, it is very well marked; in the goldfish it is very faint. The lateral line itself is heavily supplied with nerves and it is thought that it serves the fish as a sixth sense—a cross between seeing and hearing—by feeling vibrations in the water. The scales along this line are punctured by a hole through the middle, presumably so that the nerves will be actually touching the water. Some fishes, the horse mackerel is one, have the lateral scales greatly enlarged so that they resemble shields.

Fish scales are comparatively easy to mount permanently by soaking overnight in turpentine, laying them on a slide and removing as much excess moisture as possible, then mounting in Canada balsam as described in Chapter X. They make very interesting polariscope preparations; moreover, a collection of scale slides can be made with little trouble and can be added to as fresh specimens come along. In this connection it is worthy of note that most fishmongers are more than a little interested in their wares and are pleased to assist anyone else who is genuinely interested. Many scales from unusual fishes have been saved for me by fishmongers.

Whilst on the subject of 'scales' those of the butterfly and other insects come readily to mind. The remarkable colours of the butterfly are due almost entirely to the scales and the metallic and prismatic hues of many beetles arise from the same cause. The scales of the butterfly resemble a Japanese fan with a short handle. On the insect itself they lie, one overlapping the other, so that an unbroken colour pattern is evolved. If the wings of a butterfly or moth are tapped so that the scales fall on a glass slip they are ready to be examined at once; they can be made into permanent mounts by following the section on 'Dry Mounting'. The scales will be seen to possess, besides their distinctive colouring, striations and other markings. At one time such scales were used to test the quality of lenses and their 're- solving' power. In particular, for very high powers, the scales of the *Podura* (a wingless insect belonging to the Collembola or Spring-tail family) were used. If the markings were all distinct, without blurring, then the lens would pass muster. A soft brush passed over the wings of the butterfly will detach, usually, sufficient for one's needs. The unaided eye is just able to discern them as tiny motes of dust, yet there are people who are so adept at mounting they can assemble them into baskets of flowers, sometimes creating birds and butterflies that flit among the blooms; the whole ensemble, consisting of hundreds of scales of various colours, having a diameter no greater than that of a pin's head. A really good slide of this description may cost ten pounds or more, yet, apart from the unusualness of the subject and its undoubted beauty, it has no value whatever save as an example of what the human hand and eye can do.

From the foregoing brief remarks it will be seen that there are near at hand a multitude of objects that are only revealed at their true value under the microscope—it is an interesting thought that until Leeuwenhoek of Delft in the late seventeenth century perfected his lenses no one, in the whole history of the world, had seen the red corpuscles in the blood or any of the minute creatures and plants that live in the water.

There are many, many more objects in the house that can be revealed in a different light with the aid of the microscope. The object has been to show that there do exist such objects and that these, if treated in the right manner, will yield their charms to the microscopist.

Preliminary examinations, as may be gathered, require a certain amount of apparatus apart from the instrument itself, of course; glass slips, cover-glasses, mounted needles, pipettes and chemicals such as glycerine or liquid paraffin. Nevertheless, even if these are not available, one can make shift with a piece of glass (from a broken picture frame, maybe) that is roughly three inches long by one inch wide. Water, as a last resort, can take the place of glycerine, a fountain pen filler can be used as a pipette and a darning needle in lieu of the mounted variety. But something, no matter how rough, must be used for the purposes indicated.

CHAPTER III

CRYSTALS

MANY of the substances commonly used in our everyday life can, with very little trouble, be made to create moving pictures for the delectation of the microscopist. All that is required is a glass slip, some warm water and a pinch of Epsom salts. Dissolve the salts in the water, using as much as the water will stand without precipitating any, that is to say, making a 'saturated solution'. Warm the slip over a bunsen burner, spirit lamp or any kind of flame and place a drop of the solution thereon. Place the slip on the stage of the microscope and use a medium-power eye-piece and objective (say the $\frac{1}{3}$-in.) and focus on the edge of the fluid. Gradually, out of the clear liquid, arrow-shaped crystals will develop, growing, apparently, out of nothing. Crystals from other parts of the fluid will encroach on those that we are examining and form fern-like patterns, incredibly beautiful. As the slip and the fluid cools the process of crystallization will slow up and will not continue until further fluid has evaporated; to assist this we must warm the slide again. If a low-power lens is used the crystallization will appear to be very slow; on the other hand, with a high power, the crystals will seem to form too rapidly, shooting across the field at a great rate.

Success does not always crown the first attempts to watch crystals form. For some reason or other only a few will condescend to grow round the edge of the liquid, or, just as you have focused on a rapidly-growing colony and sit enthralled at the mysterious pattern that is unfolding before your eyes you call someone to have a look as well. Instead of an amazed expression spreading over their face there is one of disappointment, the crystals have ceased to form. Look as long as you will yet the performance is not repeated; the slide is left on the table whilst you attend to something else and the next time you look at it the drop of fluid has crystallized all over, behind your back, so to speak.

To attain any measure of success it is necessary, in the first place, to have as strong a solution as possible. Next, have the slide warm, but not so warm that the liquid is evaporated all at once, and spread the drop as thinly as possible. The crystals nearly always start to form at the edges, so if through surface attraction you can-

not get a thin film, slightly incline the microscope so that one edge of the drop is wedge-
shaped.

The pattern formed by Epsom salts is as beautiful as any and generally takes on a fern-like
design. If a particularly fine pattern has been
achieved that one would like to have as a permanent mount the procedure is as follows: wipe
around the crystallized drop with a clean cloth
to remove dust or smear, then place a drop of
castor oil on the crystals. Next take a cover-slip
and lay it gently over the oil and finish off as
described in the chapter on finishing and ringing.
The oil may dissolve a little of the pattern but not
enough to notice.

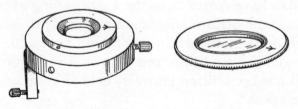

FIG. 3.—ANALYSER   FIG. 4.—POLARIZER

Such a slide is always a delight to look at and
if the microscope is fitted with a polarizer then
the delight is increased a hundredfold.

This seems to be as good a place as any to
dilate on this adjunct to the microscope so I will
give a brief description of it herewith. The

apparatus itself consists of, first, the polarizer which is fitted to the underside of the stage in place of the condenser and, second, the analyser which is inserted between the objective and the draw-tube. Usually, the objective is removed, the analyser screwed into its place and the objective screwed to the other end of the analyser. An efficient polarizer, quite suited to the needs of most students, and analyser may be purchased new for about eight pounds the two.

With this equipment a peculiar stereoscopic effect is produced and the crystals take on many prismatic colours. If a thin strip of selenite is interposed between the crystals and the objective various other colour values are obtained. Selenite is a mineral of the gypsum kind and has the property of cleaving into thin plates like mica. Several different colours are found and according to the colour used so the crystals, or whatever is being examined, are tinted accordingly. Thin plates of selenite conveniently mounted on glass slips are stocked by the leading microscope houses and cost about half a crown each.

The part of the polarizer equipment that fits into the sub-stage is capable of being revolved; this alters the position of the light rays and produces many varied and bizarre effects.

So far only one crystalline salt has been touched upon. A short foray around the house will bring to light many other substances that crystallize readily, and from the chemist, for a few pence, we can get still further material. The following list is by no means comprehensive but it contains only such chemicals as are obtainable easily and inexpensively. Mostly they are in powder form, sometimes in crystals, in any case they should be kept in airtight bottles for then they will not deteriorate and can be called on at all times.

Unless otherwise stated the following can be made to crystallize according to the instructions for Epsom salts.

Chloride of Sodium (Common salt). For preference use rock or crude salt as these give better results than the refined table salts which contain other chemicals to prevent caking.

Sulphate of Copper (Blue stone). This is a softish material, blue in colour, which, when moistened with water and rubbed over a smooth iron surface leaves a coppery tint. For this reason it is used by engineers when making diagrams on that metal. Dissolve a small piece in water and with a glass rod place a drop on a warm slide when beautiful blue crystals will form.

Sulphate of Iron (Green stone). Used by chemists in certain kinds of tonic medicine and may be obtained in large or small crystals, which, in this case, are a very pale shade of green.

Boracic Acid. This, the well-known mild antiseptic, produces rather interesting crystals provided the solution is sufficiently saturated. Leave a teaspoonful of either the powder or the crystals to stand for half an hour in an egg-cup of hot water, stirring occasionally. The resultant fluid will then crystallize readily on a warm slide.

Alum. Treat as for Boracic Acid.

Borax. As above.

Carbonate of Soda (Common washing soda). This will form crystals as readily as Epsom salts by using the same method.

Iodide of Potassium. (A form of iodine, obtainable from all chemists.) When purchased this is in liquid form, all that one has to do is to place a drop on a warm slide and await the formation of the deep, orange crystals.

Sugar. Treat as for Epsom salts, which, by the way, is also known as Sulphate of Magnesia.

Hyposulphate of Soda (the 'hypo' of the photographer). As above.

Bitartrate of Potash (Cream of Tartar). This substance is used by the cook for many things, including the manufacture of home-made lemonade. It is a crystalline formation that exists in the juice of the grape and is deposited, as such, on the

51

inside of wine casks. Cream of Tartar does not dissolve easily in water; matters are improved considerably, however, if the water is really hot.

Tartaric Acid. Very similar to the above save that a solution made from the rather large crystals as sold by the chemist readily crystallizes in many and varied shapes. Its use is, mainly, to put the fizz into health salts.

Chlorate of Potash. Pellets of this substance are obtainable from the chemist as they are used to ameliorate sore throats. Crush the pellet in warm water and proceed as with other salts.

Tartrate of Soda and Potash (Rochelle salt). This mild aperient when treated in the usual way produces very interesting eight-sided crystals.

Nitrate of Potash (Saltpetre). Proceed as with other salts.

Chloride of Ammonia (Sal-ammoniac). As above.

Sulphate of Soda (Glauber's salt). As above.

Citric Acid. Used in the making of lemonade. As above.

Permanganate of Potash. This is obtainable in deep, wine-coloured crystals from the chemist and is commonly used as a mild disinfectant or for staining woodwork. It is one of the easiest substances to make form crystals and although they are not remarkable for any bizarre shape or form, they 'grow' from the purple liquid in a very fascinating way. The crystals are rod-like and thin, like needles almost, and appear from nowhere, it seems, suddenly and unexpectedly, and no two crystals are the same length; some are short and others stretch out until you begin to wonder when they are going to desist.

Oxalic Acid. This somewhat dangerous poison is used for a number of purposes, the principal one, so far as the house itself is concerned, is that of cleaning badly-tarnished brass-work. As it forms into very beautifully arranged crystals it would be a pity to exclude it from the series. Fortunately, however, it is not necessary to run the risk of the younger members of the household inadvertently poisoning themselves for these same oxalic acid crystals are contained in the juice of the rhubarb and wood-sorrel. Squeeze a drop of the liquid that exudes from the freshly-cut stem of either of these plants on to a warm slide; when the juice begins to evaporate then the crystals will start their performance. The sap from the stems of many other plants forms different kinds of crystal when treated in the same way.

With practice the gentle art of persuading crystals to appear from the clear liquid will come easily. I know of no other branch of microscopy that is at once so fascinating, so puzzling and so

53

full of interest as this, especially when a polarizer is available.

There are many other good polarizer objects readily to hand besides the crystals already mentioned. They may be found in most gardens in the plants growing there. We have already made mention of the oxalic acid crystals in the rhubarb leaf-stem and root and in wood sorrel. These crystals are known as raphides and occur in various other plants; in all cases they are needle-shaped and arise from accumulations of insoluble salts in the plants. The milky fluid which oozes out of the dandelion stem when we cut it consists of a form of latex (in Russia they grow a special variety of this plant solely for the rubber) plus various forms of crystals.

By pressing out the sap from the cut stem of the common hyacinth, the common squill or the root of the iris, we may obtain some very beautiful raphides. The sap of the cactus also contains crystals but these have a circular, dish-like shape. Carbonate of lime forms on the surface of certain of the stoneworts as crystals. *Deutzia scabra*, one of the saxifrages, produces beautiful star-like crystals of silica on the underside of its leaves.

Both sugar and honey produce crystals which are much alike in shape except that those of the latter are thinner and altogether more delicate.

54

When the two are mixed, as they sometimes are, the sugar crystals lose their sharp outline.

Starch is another excellent polarizing object and it is present in many vegetable tissues. If we are in any doubt as to whether the vegetable matter we wish to treat contains starch granules, we apply a drop of iodine solution to a thin section of it. If starch is present the iodine solution will turn the granules a deep blue; no other substance gives the same reaction to that solution.

Starch is insoluble in water, so if we crush the vegetable matter to a pulp in a mortar and tip the contents into a jar of water and stir it the starch will float in the water. It can then be poured off and allowed to precipitate and then be drawn off with a pipette and examined.

Rock sections, especially those of crystalline rocks make really interesting subjects for the polarizer. They may be purchased from firms dealing in microscope slides but they are rather expensive. When we come to try our hand at making these sections we can appreciate why, although the professional mounter of such sections uses a lapidary's wheel, the cost is so high.

However, as a start let us first try our hand at a fairly soft 'rock', although we may get somewhat blackened in the attempt. Coal is the rock I am referring to and it is as well to make our initial mistakes on this easily worked substance as on the lengthy and laborious job of reducing such rocks as granite to a wafer thinness.

First of all we must chip off a piece of the coal as thinly as possible, which is then cemented to a stout glass slip, say about two inches square and an eighth of an inch in thickness. One of the best cements for this purpose is Canada balsam warmed in a spoon and dripped on to the glass; the sliver of coal is pressed gently on to the balsam and left until the balsam has set. Very gently the coal is rubbed over a sheet of glass or steel on which is medium emery powder and water. After a while that surface should be flat, then it should be rubbed on fine emery and water and finally, when the surface is sufficiently polished, the glass should be placed under a gentle flow of water from the tap, to remove dust, etc.

We now take an ordinary three inches by one inch glass slip and place on its centre a smear of balsam. By gently warming the slip holding the piece of coal the balsam will melt. Press the side of the new slip on which the balsam is, on to the flattened surface of the coal, and by this means it will be transferred with the unground side uppermost. The process of grinding first with the coarse emery and then with the fine, or flour, emery and water is repeated, and this is where we land into all kinds of exasperating difficulties. Either we overdo the grinding and the hoped-for section of coal is so thin and fragile that it disintegrates or we do not get it quite thin enough. In any case, I am sure that before you arrive at anything like success you will have called me every possible name you can think of for putting the idea into your head. When you come to trying it out on crystalline and other hard rocks you will certainly be exasperated, especially if after hours of patient toil the wretched section decides to misbehave itself.

But let us suppose our efforts have not been wasted. On the glass slip there is a thin section of coal or rock. Rinse it well under the tap and dry at room temperature. Put a drop of Canada balsam on the section and gently press a previously warmed cover-slip over it and lightly press it down with a needle. When all is set hard the excess balsam may be removed with xylol.

The coal section may, or may not, reveal its vegetable cells but, at least, like the sections of the harder rocks, it makes a good subject for the polarizer.

CHAPTER IV

VEGETABLE FIBRES AND ANIMAL HAIRS

DOMESTIC pets and farm animals will provide a start in our study of animal hairs—cats, dogs, rabbits, guinea-pigs, hamsters, mice, rats, squirrels, horses, cows, donkeys, sheep, pigs, etc. The mole, hare, the various field and water relations of the mouse, the deer, fox, badger and the otter are occasionally encountered in our walks abroad. For the townsman there is the zoo. At moulting time tufts of hair may be found attached to the wire of the enclosure and a friendly keeper might be persuaded to obtain hair from the cages of the less accessible inmates.

It will be seen, then, that a good, named collection may be thus acquired at very little expense and you will be able to tell whether milady's fur coat originally covered a pussy-cat or a rabbit—or a silver fox.

Identification depends largely on the size and nature of the three principal cell-layers forming the hair itself. First there is, right in the middle, the medulla or 'marrow' which may be absent or

58

vestigial in very fine hairs, such as certain wools or very thick as in bristle-hairs. The middle layer is called the cortex, the cells of which vary in length according to the species but are always parallel to the longitudinal axis. Next is the epidermis which may, or may not, consist of four layers; generally, however, it is referred to as the 'scale' consisting, usually, of a pattern of scales lying flat along the hair. In some hairs, notably those of the long-eared bat, the scales stand away from the cortex.

To examine the medulla the hair should be mounted in benzene when it will appear dark against the other cells. Otherwise, for immediate examination a drop of glycerol or liquid paraffin is placed on a glass slip and the hair laid in it. For permanent mounts euparal should be used as it does not make the scale margins indistinct as does Canada balsam.

I have remarked that the diameters of the medulla and of the hair itself are identifying factors of hairs, and as the identification of many other objects relies largely on their size it would, perhaps, be as well if I dealt with measuring with the microscope. This seems to be as good a place as any to do this.

First we shall require an eye-piece micrometer, and this consists of a plain glass disc, 21 mm. in diameter, in the centre of which are a number of equally-spaced divisions. The top lens of the eye-piece is unscrewed and the glass disc is dropped into the eye-piece; it will be held in position by an internal ring which is part of the complete lens. The top lens is then screwed back into place. When we look through the micro-scope now we shall see, superimposed on the object, the lines of the divisions magnified accord-ing to the power of the lens used. If it is a hair that we are looking at we turn the eye-piece round until the scale is at right angles across the hair; then the slide is moved until the first division of the scale touches one edge of the object. Thus we can count the number of divisions occupied by the diameter of the hair.

So far so good, but we have not yet any stan-dard measurement to go by, only the number of scale divisions. It is necessary, therefore, to cali-brate the eye-piece micrometer first, and having once calibrated it we can use it for measuring other microscopic objects, such as diatoms, cells, pollen grains, etc. To calibrate it a stage micro-meter is used. This is a glass slip divided into either inch or millimetre fractions. The inch will be in thousandths of an inch with the hundredths divided off by a longer line; the millimetre scale is in hundredths and tenths of a millimetre. The standard of measurement for microscopic objects is the micron, indicated by the Greek letter mu (μ), and it represents a millionth part of a metre. Therefore each of the 0.01mm. divisions equals ten microns.

However, we look down the microscope and turn the eye-piece round until the first division of its scale is superimposed on the first division of the stage micrometer. Thus each division of the eye-piece micrometer can be gauged by the number of stage micrometer divisions it covers or, in the case of high magnifications, the number required to encompass one of the stage divisions. In order to get a workable number of eye-piece divisions into an equally workable number of stage divisions it may be necessary to extend the draw-tube a little. Naturally, the draw-tube should be marked at the appropriate place and extended to that mark whenever measuring is to take place. Also the same lenses must be used.

Assuming that ten eye-piece divisions cover twenty stage divisions exactly, then we know that each of the former measures 200 microns divided by 10, that is, 20 microns per division. A note should be made of the calibration of each different combination of lenses and kept in the case with the microscope.

Vegetable Fibres

In the first place, these have absolutely nothing in common with animal hairs other than their elongated shape. They vary from the hairs emanating from the seeds of the cotton plant to the tough 'veins' of the stem of the flax and sisal plants, and from the fibre which forms around the coconut as a thick coating to the hair fibres from the fruit of the kapoc tree.

We have noted that animal hairs are formed of various solid layers but the plant fibre, on the other hand, is composed of numerous zones of cells containing protoplasm. This, not infrequently, shrinks to the cell-walls when the fibre is dried. These fibre cells differ slightly from cells from elsewhere in the plant, for they are elongated and have thick walls and, in consequence, the centre part is considerably reduced. This also helps to make the fibre tough and capable of being spun into a long thread as is done with cotton hairs and flax fibres, or twisted into string or rope as with ramie (a member of the nettle family), hemp, sisal, etc.

Vegetable fibres should be examined dry first, that is, placed on a glass slip and covered with another slip or cover-glass. In this way the outer structure can be seen clearly, but not that of the interior. After this it should be placed on another slip with a drop of water and a cover-glass laid over it—this will keep the curly fibres under control. We can now examine the interior. The air in the cells will probably give rise to many air-bubbles which will undoubtedly mask the details we wish to see. If a drop of commercial alcohol, diluted to 96%, is placed under the cover-glass and drawn through by touching the water at the other side with a piece of filter or blotting paper, the bubbles should disappear.

We now come to the stage where we have examined our fibres by the methods just mentioned and wish to make permanent mounts of them. But before we do this let us first consider the structure of the cell-wall of the vegetable fibres.

The cell-walls of plants vary considerably in their chemical composition; many, especially young cells, contain cellulose; others contain pectins, hemicellulose, silica (as in the epidermis of many grasses) or lignin; this last, the woody part of otherwise soft tissues, is partly responsible for the strength of commercial fibres.

Some stains affect one type of cell composition and some, others. Thus, gentian violet will readily dye cellulose but it only gives to lignin a very faint colouring. Safranine stains lignified

PLATE IV

INSECT SCALES AND *MYCETOZOA*

Scales.

1. Scale of White Moth.
2.   ,,   ,, Privet Hawk Moth.
3.   ,,   ,, Gnat (body).
4.   ,,   ,, White-lettered Hairstreak.
5.   ,,   ,, Common Blue.
6.   ,,   ,, 6-spot Burnet.
7.   ,,   ,, Swallow-tail Butterfly.
8. Bristle plumule of Grizzled Skipper.
9. Tufted plumule of Satyr.
10. Scale of *Polyommatus argus* (Azure blue). × 400.
11.   ,,   ,, Cabbage White.
12.   ,,   ,, Emperor Moth.

Mycetozoa.

These illustrations are of the sporangia of a kind of fungus which has some of the characteristics of the lower forms of animal life. They are found on rotting wood and decaying leaves in the dank parts of woods and forests. The sporangia stand out from the main body or plasmodium and are just visible to the unaided eye.

13. *Lepidoderma Tigrinum.*
14. *Cribraria Languescens.*
15. *Diachaea leucopoda.* × 25.
16. *Areyria denudata.* × 8.
17. *Stemonites fusca.* × 7.
18. *Dictydium cancellatum* var. *fuscum.* × 56.
19. *Prototricha metallica.* × 20.
20. *Cratevium minutum.* × 50.

64

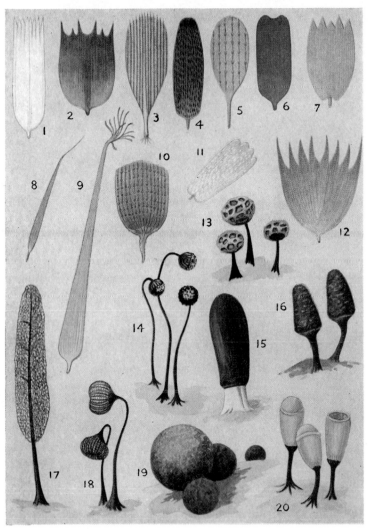

Plate IV

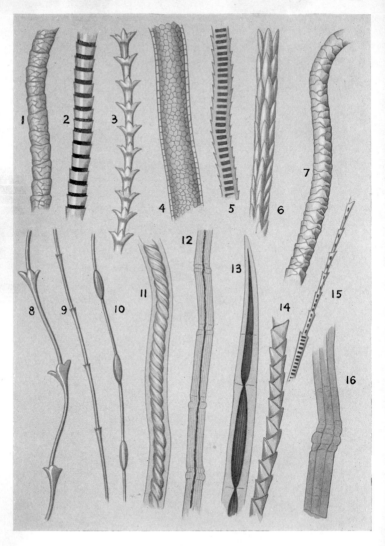

Plate V

PLATE V

HAIRS AND FIBRES

1. Hair of Camel (*Camelus bactrianus*).
2. „ „ Rat.
3. „ „ Indian Bat.
4. „ „ Moose (*Cervus alus*).
5. „ „ Badger (*Meles taxus*).
6. „ „ Kangaroo (*Macropus*).
7. „ „ Sheep (Merino).
8. Down of Eider Duck.
9. „   „ Goshawk.
10. „   „ Tawny Owl.
11. Fibre of Cotton.
12. „ „ Flax.
13. „ „ Jute.
14. Hair of Bat (*Vespertilis pipistrellus*).
15. „ „ Shrew (*Amphisorex rusticus*).
16. Fibre of Hemp.

E

cellulose a dark red but when lignin is not present it only stains a pale red. A solution of picric acid in alcohol stains proteins yellow.

There is also a sort of general utility stain which is produced by the Shirley Institute of Manchester and marketed by I.C.I. which is very obliging in the way it stains a variety of different fibres in distinctive colours. It is particularly useful in assessing the composition of paper. It is called shirlastain and will dye flax a brownish purple, ramie it will dye a lavender colour, cotton a pale purple, sisal and jute a golden brown; kapoc (and wool) yellow and pure silk brown. Yes, one can get a lot of fun from fibres and shirlastain.

CHAPTER V

POND life microscopy has a fascination entirely its own. It presents a new world to the viewer, a bustling world of small organisms each with its own problems and particular mode of life. Moreover, the enthusiast does not have to go far to find his material; the water-butt in the garden, the lily-pool, the wayside duck-pond, the lake and reservoir all provide tiny forms of life, many of which are beautiful, and all of which are interesting. The stream, river, canal and even the ditch, stagnant though it may be, can supply a rich harvest of queer little creatures and unplantlike plants.

But first of all, having found the piece of water we wish to investigate, we have to remove them from their habitat and then so arrange matters that we can examine them, either in their living state or as mounted preparations. In order to achieve this we shall require implements of various types, none of which, incidentally, need be of an elaborate nature. Even the least handy of people can contrive something or other to meet each particular need, whilst for the serious student of the subject there are numerous firms who can supply the necessary equipment.

Perhaps the most simple method of obtaining the weed-loving organisms is to detach a clump of weeds with the crook of a walking stick, and putting it in a clean jar (jam or otherwise) fill it up with water from the same pond or stream. Duckweed forms a very interesting subject, especially when low-powers are used; it also harbours many small creatures. Unfortunately, it is difficult to get it to leave the stick owing to its clinging nature.

The weedy material so collected may later be placed in a shallow dish; the weed will gradually spread out in the water and the inhabitants will soon pursue their normal way of living. The copepods and water-fleas will dart about restlessly, likewise the small insects. Many organisms will not leave the shelter of the weed and many of the minute kind will also be invisible to the unaided eye. A small portion placed with some water in a watch-glass may be examined with a low-power. The tendency is to move the watch-glass about on the stage, especially when some interesting-looking creature wanders out of the field; but I find, in the long run, that it is better to wait until it decides to wander into view again. With practice such wanderers can be transferred to the more restricted space of an excavated slide, and if a few strands of blanket-weed (or teased out cotton wool) are also placed in the excavation to restrain its movements the creature can be thoroughly examined at leisure.

A good way of obtaining a concentration of any gathering, whether from the surface, the bottom, or, as in the present instance, from weed-clumps, is to place it in a dish, the outside of which has been painted black save for one small space. Many of the small organisms are phototropic; that is, attracted by light, so these will eventually move towards the lighted area. They may then be removed *en masse* without being mixed with unwanted matter. Other organisms, on the other hand, do not like the light at all, and to deal with these one may reverse the process and use a dish with a darkened area. In both instances the movement to the selected area is not a rapid one and it may take a couple of hours before some of the smaller organisms get there.

Very often it so happens that the enthusiast is walking in the country and comes across a very promising-looking pool but does not happen to have any collecting equipment with him, not even a glass jar. He need not go away empty-handed;

a clump of weed can be taken from the water and wrapped in several thicknesses of newspaper and placed in a jar of water on returning home. A great many organisms will be retained and quite a number of them will have survived in the damp weed.

Needless to say all material, no matter by what means it is collected, should be dealt with as soon as possible, or the larger creatures will devour the smaller ones before you have a chance to look at them. If it is obvious that many hours must elapse before the gathering can be examined, then it should be killed (and also preserved) by adding formalin to the water.

The aforementioned 'hit or miss' methods of collecting, although serving their purpose, leave the greater part of the water unexplored. To make a really thorough investigation of the minute inhabitants of the water various types of equipment are necessary.

For water mites, tiny insects, and the like, a form of sweep net is used. This can be readily constructed at

FIG. 5.—COARSE NET FOR USE AMONG THE STEMS OF REEDS, ETC.

home from a length of stout wire or thin metal rod bent into a circle and the ends fixed into the end of a cane or wooden pole. A long tapering net is attached to the loop. Muslin or, better still, coarse meshed silk will serve for the net. At the apex a test tube should be inserted and

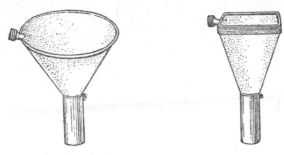

FIG. 6.—FINE SWEEP NETS: NOTICE DETACHABLE CONTAINER ATAPEX

into this the catch will congregate. The net is swept several times through the water or on the surface and the tube removed.

For the small organisms of the mid-water area (the plankton) we shall need a plankton net. This is a similar appliance to the net just mentioned except that it has a longer and more tapering bag, and the mouth is not attached directly to the handle. This net can be used from the side of the lake or pond if a stout rod, six feet or so in length, say, is attached to the bridles at the net opening. The net can then be swept through the water;

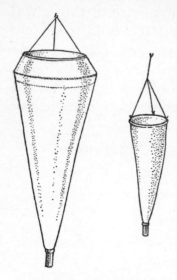

FIG. 7.—FINE NETS FOR CAPTURING MID-WATER SPECIMENS

the depth at which it will work will be governed mostly by the pace at which the net is moved. On large expanses of water the net can be towed behind a boat. Here the net may have to be weighted fore and aft if deep water samples are to be obtained. In the stream or river it can be operated from a bridge; the current will be sufficient to 'fish' it. An alternative to the tow-net is sometimes used when investigating the micro-flora and fauna at specific depths in deep lakes; a small pump on a boat draws water through a hose pipe that has been lowered to the required depth. The water thus raised falls into a plankton net suspended over the side of the boat, the water passes through the net, and the catch is accumulated in the usual tube at the apex of the net. By this means samples can be taken from a number of known depths, and it is especially useful for tracing the vertical movements of the plankton— movements actuated by the time of the day, the

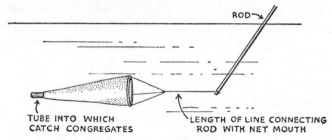

TUBE INTO WHICH
CATCH CONGREGATES

LENGTH OF LINE CONNECTING
ROD WITH NET MOUTH

FIG. 8.—FINE NET IN USE IN MID-WATER

season of the year, the weather, the temperature and the condition of the water.

For samples from the bed of a pond or, in particular, a lake, a stout, heavy dredge with an iron frame and canvas body is used and this, too, is towed behind a boat. At the 'cod' end or apex of the net a 'tangle' is sometimes used to advantage and this consists of a few pieces of teased-out rope in the midst of which some hooks of assorted sizes have been fixed. The tangle can also be used advantageously from the bank, and indeed it is a good plan to make a tangle especially for this purpose. The frayed-out pieces of rope can be affixed at intervals to a short length of iron bar or tubing with a bridle connecting the two ends. If the rope is long enough this contraption can be thrown quite a distance over the water. The materials so obtained from the bottom should be deposited on a mackintosh sheet. They will give a good picture of the bed itself which will vary greatly according to the type of water and the season of the year. The catch can be sieved for the larger organisms and the residue placed in a jar for later examination and study.

From the sand or mud of the shallows and from the edge of the water a rich haul is usually obtained, particularly from the surface layers. There is no necessity for equipment of an unduly elaborate nature in any of our types of collecting and so, for the edge uncovered by water, an old tablespoon will suffice. A thin layer of the surface should be scraped up and placed in a labelled jar to be examined later in a petri dish. To collect a sample of soil from the shallows an ordinary fish slice takes a lot of beating, especially the kind that is used sideways. It is used in the same manner as the spoon and the holes enable the water to run away. Some organisms live deep down in the mud, and so a trowel or even a spade is necessary to get at them. This mud can be washed through a sieve the mesh of which will determine the size of organisms to be retained.

Next there are the organisms of the shallows to be attended to and, first of all, stones should be scrutinized for bryozoa, algae, etc., likewise the piles of piers and landing-stages, and partly submerged trees and their roots. The stems of aquatic plants should be searched for molluscs, crustaceans, eggs of various creatures, diatoms and rotifers. It is amongst the roots, however, that one finds the juvenile fishes, amphipods, isopods and other small fry. A small, sturdy net is necessary here, and in order to get between the roots and stems of close-packed plants a triangular net is the best. It should have the frame made of iron or steel rod not less than $\frac{3}{8}$-in. diameter with each of the three sides about eight inches long. The net itself should be made of stout cloth, otherwise the sharp stones or snags will soon tear it. Likewise a thin cane handle is next to useless, that is, if the net is to be used with sufficient vigour to get well into the nooks and crannies. A bamboo rod, half an inch or more in diameter or, failing that, a broomstick about five feet long is advisable. The bag of the net need only be about five inches deep and will not require an attached tube—it only gets tangled in the undergrowth. The net is generally used by jabbing sharply between the stems and weed masses and after each jab it is turned inside out into a wide-mouthed jar of water. The catch taken in this way is ideal for observation in a small aquarium and in this connection almost any kind of disused glassware may be utilized, even flat potted-meat jars.

75

There remain two further methods of collecting to be considered in order to obtain a satisfactory survey of the aquatic life in pond or stream. At night one may shine a light on the water and then, after about an hour, run a sweep net through the illuminated area. This often results in a haul of the more retiring organisms which, attracted by the light, rise to the surface.

Finally, there are the stems and leaves of such plants as water-lilies, sagittaria, villarsia, etc., to be examined, that grow at some distance from the bank. The stems must be cut off and brought ashore, a distance at times of fifteen feet or more. Let it be said at the onset that it is practically impossible to cut through a lily stem with a knife, be it never so sharp, tied at the end of a pole— the stem just wanders away from it. A 'V'-shaped implement that can be tied to the end of a rod is by far the best—it could be made by a blacksmith or purchased from one or other of the firms that deal in collecting equipment. In particular, the undersides of the larger floating leaves should be searched over carefully, preferably with a large hand-magnifier.

Whatever methods of collecting are used it is well to bear in mind that a survey of one part of a pond or lake, or one particular reach of a river or stream, is not necessarily a complete picture of the whole—different parts yield different material.

And now for some of the things we shall expect to find in our gathcrings and of how we must treat them in order to see them clearly under our microscope.

First of all the gathering should be placed in a petri-dish and the larger organisms removed with a pair of forceps and put into a watch glass, containing water, to be examined separately and, of course, to be mounted later. The small, remaining plants and animals should be examined under a low-power for the more active kinds; then a higher power should be used to see the sedentary kinds. A glass slip should be kept handy so that anything particularly interesting which we want to put aside either for study under a high-power or for a mounted preparation may be removed with a finely-pointed pipette and placed thereon.

This at first is by no means an easy operation; the image being reversed makes matters difficult, but in time one becomes used to it. Moreover, no matter how fine the point of the pipette is it looks gigantic when magnified and this magnification also affects movement—the slightest tremor will move the point right away from the object. Practice overcomes these obstacles in time but the beginner, at first, finds them irritating.

77

After studying the catch in its living state it can be killed and preserved by adding formalin to make, roughly, a 2% solution.

At one time all the minute organisms—flagellates, ciliates, diatoms, rotifers, etc.—were lumped together under the convenient heading of infusoria because they were thought to be 'generated' by boiling hay and other vegetable matter and allowing the infusion to cool. It was believed that these minute beings were actually created within the infusion. Now, of course, we know that the infusion is merely the food upon which the airborne minutiae thrive. The name has remained. It is a convenient one and embraces most of the lowly groups of pond life.

ALGAE

Sea-weeds belong to this very large phylum of non-flowering plants, but it would be rather difficult to refer to the pond kind as 'fresh-water seaweeds', so we must content ourselves with the Latin word *Algae*, which means sea-weeds.

The freshwater kind fall into two rough groups; those in which the cells tend to be joined end to end to form long, thin filaments, such as *Spirogyra*, *Conferva*, *Ulothrix*, *Oedogonium* and so forth, and those in which the cells are either separate as in

Euglena, *Chlamyodomonas*, etc., or in small colonies, such as *Pandorina* and some of the *Volvoces*.

The filamentous algae are familiar enough to the pond-keeper, he calls them 'blanket weeds', from the blanketing effect of the filaments. Vexatious though it is to the man who likes to see his pond neat and tidy, when examined under the microscope the strands are really delightful to see —and study. A piece may be kept in a small jar of water (even a potted-meat jar will do); it will soon grow and then one may watch the various phases in the life histories of the different species. Reproduction is either by cell-division or by two cells conjugating. This latter results in a special form of cell which eventually bursts, and out swarm a number of minute oval bodies which, propelled by flagella, swim around until they assume the parent form.

The most satisfactory way of viewing the filamentous types is to place a few strands on a glass slip with a drop of water and cover them with a thin cover-slip. The strands are kept under control (some, like fibres, tend to curl) and the various kinds of cell structure can be examined. They are best preserved as a fluid mount.

Many of the really minute algae are difficult to see very well in their living state; they just go weaving about in the water and never seem to

Plate VI

DIATOMS

1. *Epithemion turgida.*
2. *Eunotia tetradon.*
3. *Diatoma vulgaris.*
4. *Surirella splendida.*
5. *Amphipleura pellucida.*
6. *Auliscus sculptus.*
7. *Fragillaria capucina.*
8. *Endictya oceanica.*
9. *Dimeregramma distans.*
10. *Hydrosera compacta.*
11. *Asterionella formosa.*
12. *Syncyclia salpa.*
13. *Actinoptychus undulatus.*
14. *Hydrosera triquetra.*
15. *Meridion circulare.*
16. *Synedra capitata.*

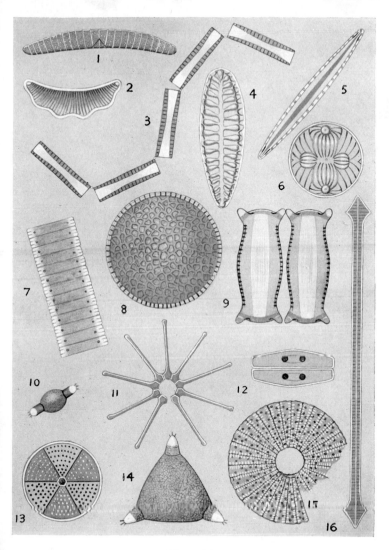

Plate VI

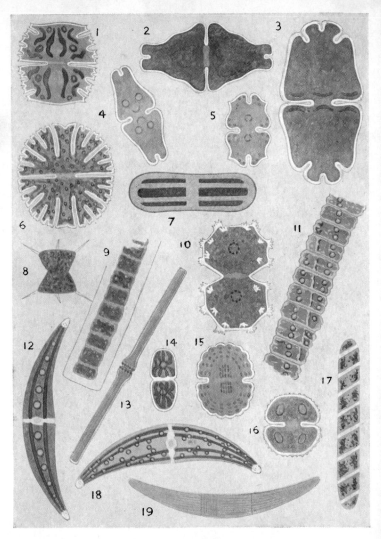

Plate VII

Plate VII

DESMIDS

1. *Micrasterias truncata.* × 200.
2. *Euastrum didelta.* × 430.
3. *Euastrum crassum.* × 400.
4. *Euastrum ansatum.* × 520.
5. *Euastrum elegans.* × 600.
6. *Micrasterias denticulata.* × 200.
7. *Penium Brebissonii.* × 400.
8. *Staurastrum dejectum.* × 500.
9. *Hyalotheca dissiliens.* × 570.
10. *Xanthidium armatum.* × 450.
11. *Desmidium Swartzii.* × 520.
12. *Closterium moniliferum.* × 400.
13. *Docidium baculum.* × 350.
14. *Cosmarium cucurbita.* × 600.
15. *Cosmarium crenatum.* × 600.
16. *Cosmarium margaratiferum.* × 500.
17. *Spirotaenia condensata.* × 500.
18. *Closterium Ehrenbergii.* × 220.
19. *Closterium striolatum.* × 300.

All the above species are found in fresh water. They prefer ponds, ditches, and very slow-moving streams where the water is sweet. They do not like shady places or turbid water.

stay long enough in one place to be seen properly. In any case they are the province of the specialist and so require nothing more than a mention here. They are known generally as the nanoplankton and all are less than ten microns in length. Nevertheless, the method of isolating them from the many other organisms in the catch is of more than passing interest, especially as it can also be applied to the isolation of other minute forms of life and in particular those which like to rest occasionally on something solid.

The material is placed in a large test tube in which a thin rectangular cover-slip has been placed. After a few days the slip is removed and the best way of doing this is to bend a piece of iron wire into the shape of a hairpin and make a slight hook at the two free ends. This is then dipped into the test tube and the slip, resting on the two hooked ends, can be easily removed. The slip is then placed on an ordinary glass slide and examined under a medium-power. Naturally, there will be all kinds of things on the slip, but there should be one part at least where your organism has come to rest in fair numbers. This piece should be broken off with a pair of forceps and placed in a separate test tube containing a nutritive solution, such as Knop's. A new slip should also be added to the new tube and, in time,

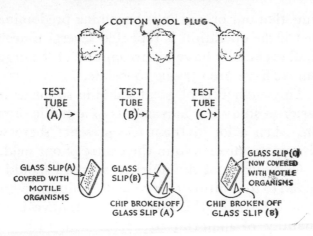

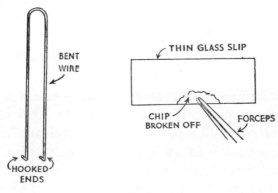

FIG. 9

the organisms contained on the sliver of glass will reproduce themselves in the nutrient medium. The new slip is then removed and examined in the same way as the first. We should find this

83

time that our organism is becoming predominant and if the operation is repeated several times we shall eventually have a pure culture of the organism we have been trying to isolate.

This method is of great value in so far as it is easier to study the movements of a motile organism when a lot of them are present; there will always be one or two in the centre of our field.

A few drops of the nutrient solution should be added to the culture every day to maintain a good growth. Also by this method we can have a good quantity of material to experiment with, and various ways of fixing and killing the organisms, so that their flagella and general shape and structure can be studied, can be tried.

Volvox is perhaps one of the most popular of all pond micro-organisms and it certainly is one of the microscopist's greatest thrills when this gorgeous organism first floats into the field of his microscope. The perfect form of each individual and the variety of ways by which they reveal their personal activities make them a veritable little world of their own, as you shall see. The plant itself is visible to the unaided eye as a pale green globule about the size of the head of the average pin. With quite a low magnification it is found to be a hollow sphere or globe of mucus apparently covered with cilia. When carmine or indigo is placed in the water the strong currents set up by these flagellae or cilia are readily seen. The result of this activity is a rolling motion which gives rise to the generic name—*Volvox*, from volvo, I revolve.

These are the cilia or filaments of the multitudinous cells or gonidia sprinkled over the interior of the mucous globe. These may be connected by strands of protoplasm which give to the whole its peculiar net-like appearance. Reproduction can take the form of new coenobia forming (a coenobium being a number of single cells contained within a gelatinous envelope) within the parent by a kind of internal gemmation or budding. One or more larger cells (up to 25) may be observed, each of which undergoes segmentation first into two and then four then sixteen equal parts until a great many tiny corpuscles have formed, and these are contained within their own coenobium. For a time they are joined by a thin membrane to the wall of the parent coenobium but after a while they cast off this 'apron string', as it were, and float freely within the parent. They are sometimes called 'daughter volvoces' and sometimes 'sister'.

So they develop and grow until there is no room left. Then they wreck the whole establishment, break through the cellular network and through the surrounding envelope and the old Volvox ceases to be a living entity. There is also a form of sexual reproduction which results in what is doubtless a 'resting' spore which may be able to withstand drought and will come to life in the spring.

Another particularly interesting feature observable at times is the presence of a rotifer, *Notommata parasitica*—very often with wife and family living quite happily within the globe of this *Volvox globator*. The adult appears to eat its way through the enveloping membrane by means of two protrusible scalpel-like teeth without causing any apparent damage. The rotifer then swims about, like a goldfish in a bowl, and seems to feed on the young *Volvoces* and on the food stored by the *Volvox* itself. When the time is ripe it breaks through the membrane again to spend the rest of its days in the surrounding water.

A fluid mount of *Volvox*, especially if infested with this rotifer, makes a very interesting preparation. A 2% solution of formalin is about as good a medium as any for this purpose.

Another interesting form is *Pediastrum*, which takes the shape of a circular, elliptic or irregular flattish frond like a plate. It is found in small pools, ditches and bogwater and makes an interesting fluid mount. The celebrated 'water-net'

86

which may entirely cover a small pool with what appears to be a green scum is a near relation. *Hydrodictyon reticulata* is the only British species and its coenobium may be a foot in length and as delicate as gossamer. To obtain a portion for a fluid mount we may have to lift some out on a glass slip, gently scrape away the unwanted part, leaving a disc with a slightly less diameter than the cell ring and then float it into a cell on another slide and then make a fluid mount of it. There are a great number of other single-celled algae and they constitute a most interesting study.

Many of the organisms which at one time were considered as being lowly animals are now quite definitely regarded as being plants. *Euglina viridis*, the tiny, roughly-oval organism that is largely responsible for water going green in the summer, is now considered as being a plant, and so too is *Codosiga*, one of the most interesting of microscopic objects. You will find this attached to the submerged leaves and stems of aquatic plants, especially those with a shaggy look. Cut off a small piece and place it in some water in a watch glass and move it so that only the edge of the leaf is in the field. Eventually you will see ghost-like bells floating out, sometimes two or more of them, according to the species. Then you will notice that they are anchored to the plant by a thin stalk and this, at the slightest vibration, will coil itself up so that the whole colony appears to vanish. Then, slowly it will expand again. They make a fascinating study as do the numerous other species in this group which is known generally as the 'colourless flagellates'.

Of the other algal forms of especial interest to the microscopist the Dinoflagellates are dealt with in the chapter on marine life, whilst the Desmids and diatoms have a chapter all to themselves.

PROTOZOA

These are the single-celled animals of which, perhaps, the most famous is *Amoeba*, that blob of jelly, for ever changing its shape, which glides over plant stems and stones either in the water or at the edges. Also found amongst the leaves of submerged plants is the spectacular relation of *amoeba*, *Actinophrys sol*. It is about a hundredth of an inch in diameter and has similar habits to its relative, but instead of the pseusopodia being shapeless, they are stiff and give a radiating sun-like appearance to the organism.

Slightly larger and even of slightly more spectacular appearance is *Actinosphaericum* which lives amongst the Duckweeds on the surface of the water. Although with a soft covering, like *amoeba*, when it encysts for the winter it develops a hard siliceous coat such as that worn by foraminifers and *Radiolaria* (these are dealt with in their own chapter). In fact, the more advanced amoeboid types possess hard coverings of some kind or another.

Actinophrys sol, white, semi-opaque and about one thousandth of an inch in diameter, is always a delight to the pond microscopist. The Sun Animalcule, as it is sometimes called, is so full of vacuoles that one gets the impression that it is composed entirely of bubbles. Numerous radiating tentacles, like the rays of the sun, give rise to its popular name. These are sticky and their main function is to entrap the small organisms on which it feeds. It is found in lakes, ponds and slow-moving streams, usually in the vicinity of confervae masses.

An organism that can be well likened to an *Actinophrys* on a stalk is the beautiful *Clathrulina elegans*. It may be found with the stalk attached to the rootlets or the underside of duckweed leaves in shady ponds. The shape is that of a sphere punctured by a number of largish openings through which protoplasmic rays protrude. This species is one of the very few freshwater radiolarians, and had not been generally recognized as a British species until some eighty years ago when it was found in Wales and Ireland. It is specimens such as *Clathrulina* popping up unexpectedly on the stage of the microscope that make glad the heart of the pond hunter.

The Ciliate Protozoa are an interesting and, as yet, imperfectly known group of the animal kingdom. True, they are of microscopic size, yet some are large enough to be visible to the unaided eye —*Stentor polymorphus*, for example. The Stentors, though generally of a trumpet shape, are able to assume a variety of forms. Around the 'mouth' of the trumpet is a wreath of cilia which, in life, are continuously in motion. The body displays various colours, red, brown, black, green, blue and white. The favourite haunt is among the convervae of stagnant water, either free-swimming or attached to plants, dead sticks, stones, etc.

Another ciliate, in many ways resembling the foregoing and an equally exciting object for our microscope, is the Bell Animalcule. Partly for its peculiar movements and partly for its delightful shape the pond microscopist is always happy when his catch includes *Vorticella*. It is by no means rare and may be found at most times of the year attached to submerged plant leaves, sometimes in such numbers as to invest them with a shaggy, white coat. Each, however, is a separate individual reacting independently to outside influences.

The animal itself consists of a bell fringed with cilia, constantly vibrating in the process of gathering food. The stalk, at the slightest provocation, concertinas and folds up completely to stretch shyly out again in a very few moments. It is an ideal object for the live box and there is no need to remove it from its support. If one has an aquarium, specimens may often be found on the leaves of the oxygenating plants. This is very useful when we require specimens at a time when pond-hunting is out of the question.

Paramoecium has the shape of a pointed oval and for that reason is sometimes called the Slipper Animalcule. It is covered with cilia which serve the purposes of attracting food and of propelling their owner through the water. Most water samples will contain some of them.

HYDROZOA

Very few 'jellyfishes' are found in fresh water. So far as diversity of species goes, their province is the sea and they will be dealt with more fully in the chapter on marine microscopy. There are, however, three species of their kind found in this country—*Hydra viridis*, green in colour, *H. fusca*, a brownish colour, and *H. rubra* which is red in colour. The first-named is by far the most common. It is found in all forms of still or slow-moving water generally adhering to stones or to vegetation by means of a sucker-like foot or hanging from the surface film by that same foot. The length may be half an inch when fully extended, but when it is alarmed it will shrink to a mere blob of jelly.

The fundamental shape is that of a tube from which several other tubes branch and at the end of the tubes are the tentacles. If a hydra taken from the pond is placed in a small glass dish it can be examined with a low-power objective. A few cyclops or small daphnia added to the water should enable one to observe the food-catching department in action.

At first all that will be seen of the hydra will be a semi-transparent blob of pale green jelly. Gradually, if undisturbed, the shapeless lump will unfold and the tentacles expand to wave gently in the water. At one end of the column the foot will be observed and at the other the tentacle-fringed mouth. The tentacles twine and weave about as though actually searching for food which, indeed, is exactly what they are doing. They are liberally sprinkled with stinging cells so that, when they embrace some lively little organism it can be stilled before being thrust down the opening that passes for a mouth in the hydroids.

THE INHABITANTS OF THE DETRITUS

I have preferred to refer to the tiny crawling creatures which inhabit the detritus of the bottom by the above title. Many are of the great 'worm' phyllum but a great many belong to other groups of the animal kingdom. All are interesting and few move with that irritating speed that is so exasperating when viewing such restless creatures as *Cyclops* and most of the ciliates. Moreover, they are very easy to collect, indeed, especially if one keeps an aquarium.

At the bottom of the tank, whether we like it or not, humus will accumulate. This the good aquarist removes regularly with a pipette. So, with that same implement, we can remove some of the humus and place it on a glass slip. One glance will be sufficient to show what a rich field this humus is—a field that has received very little attention from either the professional biologist or the amateur.

For the most part they will be microscopic and have a semi-transparent appearance and will glide and slither between the solid particles of the detritus. Their shape will also be obscured by those same particles and so, to see them more clearly, they should be isolated; in any case this must be done if they are to be mounted with any degree

93

of success. To do this another slip should be placed at the side of the microscope with a drop of clear water on it. Then the individuals should be removed separately and deposited in the clear water. To do this I know of no better implement than a bristle from a well-worn shaving brush or a camel hair brush from which all save a few bristles have been removed. The specimen is lightly entangled in the frayed-out bristle and transferred to the water, remembering that any harsh treatment will probably kill the specimen or badly damage it. When the object has been observed for as long as is required it can be made into a permanent mount by mounting in fluid.

The principal forms of life to be found, apart from diatoms, desmids, foraminifera, cypris, etc., are:

The Planarians. These are flat worms and look very much like leeches and vary in size from the microscopic to about half an inch or more in length. Some species cling to the underside of stones or submerged plants, some are found near the surface of the water and quite a number inhabit the mud. The shape may be either cylindrical, thread-like, spindle-shaped or more or less flattened and leaf-like. The colour of the microscopical forms may be bright yellow, orange, red or rose. Some have a green tinge and this is due to single-celled plants living within their outer covering.

The Gastrotricha. The Gastrotricha are smaller generally than the foregoing—a specimen of half a millimetre in length is considered as being gigantic—and are by no means so brightly coloured. They move in a gliding sort of way reminiscent of the ciliates. The body is cylindrical and usually there is an expanded area in front known as the 'head', a narrower part or 'neck' and the large 'rump' or body proper. This forms the major part of the animal and half of it is occupied by eggs. Although the Gastrotricha are so prolific the male has yet to be described.

The Nematodes. These writhing, twisting little 'worms' are found everywhere, from the depths of the ocean to the most barren of deserts. They vary in length from a seventieth to three-quarters of an inch, one of the larger species being the familiar Vinegar Eel. Some crawl sluggishly over the mud or vegetation, others twist and wriggle vigorously. Some have a sucker at the tail by means of which they can anchor themselves to any solid object. All species are slender and typically worm-like in appearance.

THE WATER BEARS

Wherever there is moisture there you will find

the curious little Water Bear or Tardigrade, but for all that they are not common generally; at least, that is my experience—perhaps I have looked in the right places at the wrong time. They are parasitic, but only on vegetation so far as is known. With their long proboscis they pierce the leaves of mosses and aquatic plants and extract the juice. One of the best and easiest ways of collecting the water bear is to shake a clump of moss over a shallow dish of water. They will sink to the bottom from which they can be collected by means of a pipette. They are seen best as a fluid mount.

ROTIFERA—the Wheel Animalcules

The members of this phylum are amongst the most interesting of all microscopic organisms. For, although the diatoms offer an amazing variety of shapes and markings, the rotifer also has a diversity of colours, mannerisms and habits and an easily observed and not too complex anatomy—sufficient to add considerably to their interest as a study. For this reason rather more space is devoted to them than to the other microscopic animals, moreover the mounting methods here given for the rotifers apply to the other worm-like creatures already mentioned.

In size they are quite small, the total length varying from slightly less than one three-hundredths of an inch to one-fifteenth of an inch according to the species.

They are to be found mostly in fresh water, being most prolific in swamps, sometimes in damp moss and in the sea. Some crawl, others swim; some spend most of their time anchored to stems or twigs and others have a definite sheath or nest. Round the head region is a ciliated corona, the waving movement of which gives the impression that the crown is revolving like a wheel. The current provided by these cilia not only attracts food towards the mouth, it also projects the organism towards the food, thus saving a lot of time.

The foot is prolonged into two toes at the base of which are glands which produce a sticky mucus. This secretion can anchor the rotifer to any solid object; moreover, like a spider, it can wander away from the anchorage producing a fine thread as it goes and which it can utilize for the return journey. They may be seen at times waving about in the water at the end of such a thread seeking food.

The living creature is generally transparent and, consequently, when examined in a live box the microscope sharply reveals all the internal organs but, even a short time after death, this sharp definition becomes indistinct even if the method of killing had not produced distortion. It is possible, however, to prepare specimens so that the internal features are clearly visible when mounted as a microscope slide.

The specimens have been collected, according to their kind, from the plankton or from the leaves and stems of aquatic plants and now repose in a watch-glass of water. The object now is to narcotize, kill and finally mount them after we have observed them fully in the living state. The best method, known as Rousselet's, is as follows. A little narcotizing fluid should be added to the water; if the cilia are still functioning add a little more until they are still. The narcotizing fluid suggested by Rousselet consists of hydrochlorate of cocaine 2% solution, 3 parts; methyl alcohol, 1 part; water, 6 parts. The rotifers will sink to the bottom and should not be contracted or distorted in any way.

Most of the water is now drained off with a pipette and a few drops of 0.25% solution of osmic acid added. This will immediately kill and fix the specimen. The osmic acid must then be drawn off with the pipette and, with the same implement, distilled water introduced. After four or five washings add a 3% solution of formalin, this being a better preservative, in this case, than alcohol which has a shrinking effect on the specimen.

If too much osmic acid has been used the specimen may turn black. If this happens it should be washed with peroxide of hydrogen before being washed with the distilled water. The material should be mounted in a shallow, excavated slide.

This can be done by removing it with the pipette to the hollow in the slide with sufficient fluid to fill it. Next lay a cover-slip over the depression and press it down lightly with a needle to exude the surplus water—taking care that the material is still there. A ring of cement should previously have been applied just outside the perimeter of the cavity. The cover-slip will adhere to the cement and, when it is firmly set, it can be ringed in the ordinary way.

If one wishes to mount the material in Canada balsam, Zograf's method must be adopted. After narcotizing add osmic acid solution for from two to four minutes. When this is removed add 10% pyroligneus acid for from five to fifteen minutes and follow with several washes with distilled water, then gradually bring up to absolute alcohol. Clear in cedarwood oil and mount in either Canada balsam or gum damar.

On the other hand the mounting can be made in glycerine jelly by following Rousselet's method as far as the formalin stage. Remove to a plain glass slip, drain off as much fluid as possible and mount in the usual glycerine jelly style.

A well-mounted rotifer, especially if of the *Floscularia* family, is an acquisition to the cabinet and always a joy to behold, particularly with dark-ground illumination.

BRYOZOA—the Moss Animalcule

The members of this group are sometimes referred to as Polyzoa, but call them what you will these 'animal-mosses' are worthy of more than passing mention. They live in colonies, each individual of which is encased in a gelatinous sac within which is suspended in fluid the U-shaped alimentary canal. At one end of this is the mouth surrounded by a fringe of tentacles which can be retracted at will. Thus, when the colony is undisturbed it has a distinct mossy appearance but at the slightest hint of danger it looks just like a blob of whitish jelly. In either case the internal organs and their actions can be clearly seen when the colony is placed in a live-box.

If the colony is one that has formed on the stem of a water plant, part of the attendant stem should be removed as well. The colony may be too large for a live-box, so in that case a petri dish of suitable size may be used, and failing that the familiar potted-meat jar. When magnified the otherwise uninteresting-looking filaments will be seen to bear a number of delightful 'blooms', the petals of which wave gently in the water like miniature sea anemones. Some even have the appearance of blooms projecting from the gelatinous mass like snowdrops from a mossy bank. Indeed, the first species to be discovered in this country, the Bell Flower Animalcule (*Lophopus crystallinus*), is most aptly named and is sufficiently large as to be readily observed even with a hand magnifier.

Unfortunately, these delicate little animals are difficult to preserve in anything other than their natural state. The slightest touch of the operator's hand on the live-box is sufficient to make each member of the colony retire within itself. Alcohol or any of the preservatives will also cause them to shrink and be distorted.

Consequently, as with the rotifers, they must be narcotized before being killed by the method already described. There is, however, a cheaper narcotizing agent than chloral hydrate and that is menthol, readily obtainable for a few pence from the chemist. A few crystals of this dropped in the water are efficacious in many cases. Naturally, the polypides must be well expanded before the agent is added, a few crystals at a time. If, when the colony is touched with a needle, they do not contract it can be assumed that they are sufficiently drugged. Now drain off the fluid with a pipette and replace it with a 3% solution of formalin. This kills instantly without distortion. A portion of the colony may now be mounted as a fluid mount. But do not forget, first of all, to observe the colony well in its living state before setting out to make a preparation of it.

Summer and autumn are the best seasons for hunting out the various Bryozoan species. Mostly they will be found in sheltered places such as the underside of stones or the stems of aquatic plants where the colony remains 'put' for the rest of its life, being added to from time to time by budding. One species, *Cristatella mucedo*, likes to creep around; it also favours plants in clear ponds and has a liking for sunlight.

HYDRACARINA—the Water Mites

If, in May or June, you come across a submerged stone or plant stem stained a bright scarlet then you may be sure you have encountered the eggs of our most common water mite, *Limnochares aquatica*, one of the 250 known British species of this semi-parasitic group. Yet, although they are so well represented in our ponds and lakes, very little is really known about them.

Ordinarily one may see the adults darting

about on the surface or crawling over the plants as brightly coloured dots, generally of a red, orange or reddish orange colour or even a mixture of chocolate and cream in a variety of patterns, and varying in size from a pinhead to a quarter of an inch in diameter.

When the larvae emerge from the egg they have a finely-ridged skin and three pairs of legs. Gradually they rise to the surface and there await a host, usually an aquatic insect such as the water beetle, on which they remain as parasites until they develop their fourth pair of legs. Incidentally, there is a related land species which chooses human beings for this purpose and those who have been unfortunate to act as host for the harvest mite will know how excruciating the experience can be.

The particular species already mentioned might well be found in collections from the mud and detritus of the bottom, but the principal source of supply for most of the other species will be from tow-nettings. They may be mounted in any of the ways given for the mounting of insects. There is one variation, however: these mites live in liquid surroundings and so they can reasonably be mounted in glycerine jelly after being killed with formalin.

THE MICROSCOPIC CRUSTACEA

Comparatively speaking, our fresh waters carry a small population of crustaceans. The sea, on the other hand, is richly provided both in numbers, species and groups. In our rivers and streams only three groups are represented that are of interest to the microscopist in their entirety. It is true that the appendages of the Fairy Shrimp (*Chirocephalus diaphanus*), the Isopod (*Asellus aquaticus*), otherwise known as the Water Louse, and the Amphipod

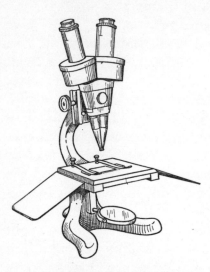

FIG. 10.—THE GREENOUGH BINOCULAR MICROSCOPE: INVALUABLE FOR DISSECTING SMALL CRUSTACEANS, ETC. THE IMAGE IS NOT INVERTED

(*Gammarus pulex*) or Water Flea, make interesting preparations. For the appropriate mounting methods, see the section on Insect Mounting.

The microscopic fresh-water crustaceans consist of three groups—the Cladocera or Water Fleas (as distinct from the other so-called 'Water Fleas'), the Ostracoda and the Copepoda.

The Cladocera. These form the only exception to the sea's monopoly of the small crustaceans. In the sea there are only five different species whereas in our British ponds and streams there are something like fifty different species.

The most common species and one well-known to the aquarist is *Daphnia pulex*, the portly, rolling little creature that seems equally at home in the puddles left by the hoofs of cattle at the water's edge as in canal or pond. A peculiar feature of *Daphnia* is its intolerance of light; during the brightest part of the day it hides away in the vegetation or mud to come out in the early morning or evening to feed.

Sometimes they are so abundant as to give the water a 'tomato chutney' appearance, at others they are particularly scarce.

The creature itself is encased in a transparent carapace with the head region protruding. Consequently the inner workings can be seen clearly and this transparency makes it a fascinating subject for the microscope. As a rule the alimentary canal can be traced as a greenish-brown thread consisting of the single-celled algae and other minutiae on which it feeds.

The head and the branched antennae protrude

from the fore-end. The eye, relatively huge, is in effect two eyes fused into one. The antennae form the only means of locomotion, consequently progression takes the form of a series of jerks. Situated just below the eye is the mouth region fringed with the powerful mandibles which deal very efficiently with its food.

Male specimens are very rarely found, not an infrequent feature amongst the smaller crustacea, and reproduction is largely parthenogenetic. The ova may be seen enclosed within the carapace where they remain until an advanced stage of development is reached; in fact, it is not unusual to find an ova within a daughter who has yet to leave the parental shelter. Broods may succeed each other at intervals of only three days or so. As a result they are ideal subjects for those who wish to trace the development and life story and to make preparations of each successive stage.

In autumn, as a result of mating, two 'resting' eggs develop. When the female moults these remain in the exuviated carapace and, as this is composed of air-cells the eggs float to the surface and so are well placed to be entangled in the feathers or feet of aquatic birds and so to be transported to other stretches of water. In small ponds which are likely to be dried up in the summer, 'resting' eggs capable of withstanding drought are produced in the spring.

There are numerous other common species of Cladocera, some of which are here illustrated.

The ideal mount is a fluid one, although glycerine jelly will also make a satisfactory preparation. When it is only the appendages one wishes to observe, then a Canada balsam mount is to be preferred.

The Ostracoda. Although visible to the unaided eye, it is not possible to make out any of the essential features of the ostracod without magnification. At first glance it might be mistaken for a tiny bivalved mollusc, but close inspection will reveal some of the appendages which we usually associate with the crustacea.

For the most part they have roughly the shape of a lentil or bean, but the size rarely exceeds that of the former, usually they are very much smaller. The 'shell' of the ostracod is a true bivalve and consists of two saucer-like halves hinged at the back. They are usually comparatively thick and hard and when closed completely encompass the rest of the animal. There is one eye situated at the fore-end of the animal. The food canal lies just below the hinge, and around the mouth are the feathery feeding appendages which collect the food—particles of decayed vegetation and algal zoospores. Behind them is a foot which is clawed and this is partly used for removing unwanted particles from the feeding appendages.

The habitat of our various species is in the mud at the bottom of lakes, pools and sluggish streams. At times, however, they may be found in the plankton of lakes.

The Copepoda. The tow-net, whether used in mid-water or near water plants, can hardly fail to gather in some at least of the copepod group. They are divided into two main kinds, the parasitic copepods which attack fishes and the non-parasitic copepods.

Although the latter kind are visible to the unaided eye one cannot see the essential features without the aid of a good hand magnifier. This will reveal the slight diversities of outline and also the various appendages, but the microscope is necessary for determining the minute differences on which identification relies.

The non-parasitic kind fall into three categories which are based on the general outline of the body:

(1) Those in which the body is a more or less elongated oval with the abdominal somites depending therefrom like a tail, the *Cyclops* type.

(2) Those in which the body is of a more robust nature and of a more or less square shape and with a shorter 'tail', the *Calanoid* type.

(3) Those in which the 'tail' follows the contour of the abdomen, resulting, as a rule, in a long, narrow worm-like creature. These are the *Harpacticids*—by far the tiniest of all the *Copepods*.

The Common Cyclops. From the head projects a pair of antennae which are nearly half the length of the body. These are fringed with hairs and form the principal means of locomotion, a series of jerks. The mouth is on the underside and this is bordered with appendages modified for the purpose of holding food matter and of conveying it to the gullet. The egg sacs are a feature of the females; there are two of them and they spread out from either side of the abdomen and are generally of a pale green colour. When the young emerge from the egg they have the resemblance of a cheese mite and it is not until there have been several moults that they look at all like the adults.

Situated at the fore-end of the head region is a single red eye (it is really two eyes fused into one) lying flush with the head. The name 'cyclops' is, of course, derived from the mythical race of one-eyed giants of that name mentioned by Homer.

Apart from sub-species, there are forty-eight different species of cyclops found in the fresh waters of this country.

The Calanoid Type. The type species of this kind is *Calanus finmarchicus*, which is common in the sea but never ventures beyond the estuaries of rivers. The most common species, perhaps, in fresh water is *Diaptomus castor* which only inhabits small pools and ditches. It is often found in the company of *Daphnia pulex* in pools that dry up in hot weather, consequently they are most prolific between September and April. Most of the other species have a preference for large lakes.

The length on an average is a tenth of an inch and the colour is variable—some specimens are dark red whilst others are a brownish-green and some may even have the segments outlined with blue—not an unusual trait in copepods at times.

In breeding and development generally this type resembles Cyclops.

The Harpacticids. A fair average length for the members of this kind is a sixty-fourth of an inch, although some are a shade larger. This small size makes their study a difficult one, especially as identification of a species may rest on the shape of the minute fifth pair of legs.

Most species prefer brackish or near-salt water; still there are sufficient species to keep the pond enthusiast busy. One of the commonest and most generally distributed fresh water species is *Canthocampus staphylinus* which is frequently to be found in weed- and leaf-choked ditches, especially amongst the debris of the bottom; such situations, indeed, as are likely to dry up in summer. Consequently, December and January see this species at its maximum although specimens can be found throughout the year.

The spring generation are of a reddish-orange colour which is due to the presence of numerous oil globules of that colour scattered throughout the body. Not infrequently they encyst themselves in the mud of the bottom throughout the summer, drawing on the oil globules for sustenance.

The Parasitic Copepods. These again fall into two groups—those that are free-swimming and can change their host when they so wish and the kind that become a permanent part of their unfortunate host. *Lepeophtheirus pectoralis* is representative of the former kind and is referred to with the rest of its kind as the Fish Louse. The other kind of which *Lernaea branchialis* is the most common attacks the gills and looks more like a worm than a crustacean. Consequently, it is known as the Gill Maggot.

Your angling friends will save infested fish for you. The free-swimming kind you will be able to remove with tweezers, but to obtain the other in its entirety it will be necessary to remove part of the branchial arch as well and then carefully dissect the head region out. Needless to say, they make interesting preparations. The best methods for making preparations are as given for *Daphnia*.

CHAPTER VI

DESMIDS, DIATOMS AND FORAMINIFERA

AT first sight there seems little reason why these
three different organisms should be lumped together in one chapter and divorced from their
more appropriate chapters. There are several
reasons, however, for this present arrangement;
one is that the diatoms are encountered not only
in the pond but in the sea as well, also they are
found in a fossil state, so it is appropriate to deal
with them separately. This also applies to the
foraminifera. The desmids are closely related to
the diatoms so they must be included with them.
Also, even though no other reason were forth-
coming, these three organisms are so bound up
in the story of the microscope and have been so
commonly beloved of microscopists for many,
many years, that it is only right that they should
have their own niche.

Moreover, various techniques and aspects of
microscopy are particularly applicable to these
organisms and they will be dealt with in this
chapter.

To start with the desmids: these, like diatoms, are unicellular plants. They are included in the algae phylum and reproduce themselves either by cell-fission or from spores. Their composition consists, roughly, of a minute speck of jelly around which a thin, though tough, skin is formed, this skin taking on a great variety of shapes according to the species. The jelly-like matter contains chlorophyll, this giving a green tint to the desmid.

Although the skin is comparatively tough the desmids are exceedingly delicate, consequently they are more than a little difficult to mount and, in any case, no matter what method is used they will lose their characteristic colour in time. A fluid mount is the most satisfactory medium, using distilled water to which a small piece of camphor has been added—this latter to prevent confervoid growths which would form within the cell otherwise. Another method is to use Deane's Medium which is used in the same way as glycerine jelly and is described in the chapter on 'Wet Mounting'.

Unless a particularly rich gathering has been acquired it is necessary to pick the desmids out, one at a time, under the microscope. Place a few drops of water from a catch known to contain them (the catch having been killed previously with weak formalin) on a glass slip. Have another slip handy; if the mount is to be a fluid one then the slip must either be of the excavated kind or have a cell ring affixed to its centre (see page 179). As it will be necessary to use high powers to observe the structure of the skin the cell must be a shallow one. This also applies to the mounting of diatoms in a cell.

The cell or excavation should be nearly filled with the mounting medium; then, with a finely-pointed sable-hair brush or a frayed-out bristle, remove each desmid to the second slip.

It is easy enough to talk glibly about picking up minutiae with brush or bristle, but I must admit at the same time that the feat is a most difficult one; it demands a sure touch, and a light one, infinite patience and the confidence that only long practice can give. Either the desmid, or whatever else is being removed, is crushed out of all recognition or the brush will gather up anything but the object desired. Even so, when the object is safely picked up it has yet to be transferred to the other slide and this, if anything, is even more difficult. The object is so small that it is well-nigh impossible to see whether the transfer has been successfully accomplished or not. In any case the brush will appear to be most reluctant to part with its cargo. A good hand-magnifier, in the absence of another microscope, is of great help in making sure that the brush has released it. Remember, too, that we are working with a low-power as we require all the space available between the object glass and the material in which to manipulate our tools. The more lightly the object is picked up the easier it is to release. Surface attraction will cause the desmid to fly away from the brush point as soon as it touches the water on the first slide. To prevent this have as little water as possible on the slide; allow a minute or so to elapse, so that the desmids will precipitate themselves, and then tilt it somewhat, when the greater part of the water will drip off one of the corners; the desmids, once precipitated, will not be washed off. Only a thin film of water will remain and this will not hinder the brush, which can now remove the object with as light a touch as you like; the object, adhering so lightly to the bristles, is easily released.

It is an interesting fact that after a while the eye becomes used to dealing with tiny things, and organisms at first entirely invisible can later be seen, if not clearly, at least sufficiently well to be picked out without the aid of a microscope.

By some means, a secret still jealously guarded by the desmid (although some authorities say they know the full answer), it is capable of a slight movement which may consist merely of turning thoughtfully on its axis or of meandering slowly towards the light. With careful focusing there will be seen in some species (principally those of the *Closterium* class) a 'cyclosis'; that is to say, a circular movement of a stream-like nature closely resembling the sap rising in a plant stem, but in this instance the 'stream' follows the outline of the individual. The skin, or tunic, is slightly elastic which, in some instances, may be seen to have a slight pulsating action. Nevertheless, the complete absence of cilia or hairs or any other means of locomotion makes their perambulations a very mysterious business indeed.

At this point I would like to digress very slightly to refer to another strange type of locomotion observable in microscopic objects and which might have some bearing on the movements of the really tiny desmids and diatoms. I am referring to the phenomenon known as Brownian movement.

This consists of erratic zig-zag movements by minute particles when suspended in liquid and which are caused by the particle being bombarded by the molecules of the surrounding fluid.

Any rock or metal, even, no matter how heavy, can be affected in this way if reduced to a sufficiently fine state. This most interesting phenomenon can be observed, however, without any great effort on our part provided we choose a very light substance to start with. The colour gamboge is of a light nature and if a cake of the water-colour variety is rubbed on a drop of water on a glass slip and covered with a cover-glass this Brownian movement will be readily visible. The student should make himself familiar with this inorganic sort of movement so that he can discriminate between it and other forms of movement, such as that of spores liberated from a swarm-cell.

To see it at its best a piece of pumice stone should be reduced to a powder in a mortar (or by any other means) and placed on a glass slip on which is a drop of water, and the whole covered by a cover-slip. If the pumice stone has been sufficiently pulverized the movement will be seen to go on indefinitely. It is said that the minute particles suspended in the contents of the fluid cavities in the quartz of the oldest rocks have been thus on the move ever since the rocks were formed aeons ago. The very fine particles of clay and the granular contents of crushed pollen grains also reveal this most fascinating movement. So far as I can see it is the nearest thing to perpetual motion.

DIATOMS

Diatoms differ but little from desmids. There are, it is true, a far greater variety of designs in the diatoms, but they lack the delicate green tint that is so delightful a feature of the desmid. The colour of the diatom varies from a dull yellow to a brownish-green; where green is the only colour it is usually rather harsh. The principal difference lies in the shell or tunic; this, in the desmid, is soft and tough, in the diatom it is hard and glassy, being composed largely of silica.

Consequently it is easier to 'clean' diatoms as they are capable of withstanding more stringent treatment. The shells are perforated as a rule, allowing the jelly-like matter which constitutes the interior of the cell to ooze through somewhat, and so a great quantity of flocculent matter adheres to the catch; therefore, in preparing a gathering for examination, not only must the ordinary detritus such as sand be removed, but the diatoms themselves must be cleaned.

Assuming, then, that we have made a haul with the net, or mud scraping, containing a fair proportion of diatoms and other organisms; what we are aiming at doing is to separate the organic matter from the inorganic matter. One way of doing this is to place the gathering in a large petri dish or glass dish such as milk puddings are cooked in, the outside of which has been painted black all save a small area at the side. If this is placed in a good light the organisms with a preference for the light will gradually move to the undarkened area; they may then be removed with a pipette. On the other hand, some have a decided preference for the dark; this being so, after waiting for a few hours for the light-lovers to assemble and after they have been transferred per pipette to a jar of clean water, the remaining material should be placed in a dish which has paint on only a small area. If the dish is so placed that the dark side faces the light the organisms which prefer the shade will gradually migrate in that direction. These can then be transferred to their fellows in the clean water.

When we have examined the living material thoroughly, formalin should be added to give a 3% solution in order to kill and preserve it. This painted dish method does not always work, some organisms could not care less whether they are in the light or in the shade, and so we must move on to the next operation. This operation, that of decanting the fluid in which the specimens are, must also be used even for the material obtained by the first method.

For this we shall require about four tallish glass

jars, and into the first of these we pour the catch. Allow the heavier particles to settle and pour off the remaining matter into the next jar. Repeat the operation with yet another, and another, jar and allowing longer and longer for each successive precipitation. When the four (or even more) jars have been refilled with water and allowed to stand for a few hours the fluid should be poured off into yet another and larger jar, preferably one of the measuring glass kind as used by chemists.

The water may look clear enough to drink, but remember the diatoms are very small indeed, even the largest are just visible as specks in the water, like motes in a sunbeam, and so they may remain in suspension for some time, especially the very tiny ones. The water in the final jar should be allowed to stand (covered over to keep the dust out) for twenty-four hours at least. A thin film will then be noticed on the bottom of the jar; this should contain the smallest of the diatoms. To get at them there is yet one more operation. Very carefully siphon off nearly all the water, save for about an inch at the bottom; swill this around a bit and then put it into a small glass. If a measuring glass is used we should be able to remove the material with a pipette.

To return to our original precipitations. From each of the jars, whilst the material is settling down, some of the fluid should be examined under the microscope in case any larger species are present. In fact, if the catch was at all rich in diatoms then we are pretty certain to find some, at least, in each decanting.

You may be thinking that it is all a tiresome business and hardly worth the candle. But there is nothing difficult about any of the operations and I can assure you there is a real thrill in reducing a handful of mud from the beach or the bottom of a pond to a collection, small though it may be, of diatoms free from all unwanted matter and bright and shining as a new pin.

The thing we are going to do now is to boil each of the precipitations for about five minutes. This may entail pouring the well-shaken precipitation into a receptacle that will withstand heat. Boil for five minutes and allow to stand for half an hour. Pour off the discoloured water and refill with clean water and boil again and repeat the process until the water is perfectly clear even after boiling. We should now have several jars each containing divers grades of sand and diatoms, both as clean as it is possible for either to be.

At intervals during the operations, a few drops of the material should be examined to make sure the diatoms are not being distorted. If the diatoms are of a robust type, three or four drops of sulphuric acid may be added to the water before boiling. Incidentally, if we are extracting the diatoms from diatomaceous earth or guano, we may use these same methods.

However, we have now arrived at the final hurdle, that of separating the diatoms from the sand. (With midwater collections there may not be any sand present at all, and the boiling will have eliminated the other organic matter.) The point to remember is that the diatoms will have lost most of their weight in the boiling process by the jelly of their interiors being dissolved away, but the sand will still have the same weight. So if the matter is well shaken and allowed to stand for only a few minutes and allowed to settle the supernatant fluid will contain nothing but diatoms. This should be run off into another jar, formalin added to 3% and the jar corked, then the gathering can be examined or mounted at leisure.

One of the principal reasons why diatoms are so popular with microscopists is that they may be found in practically any kind of water—the sea, estuaries, creeks, salting pools, lakes, ponds, and slow-moving streams everywhere. The student at the seaside can at certain times obtain a fair gathering of various species without having to use any equipment whatever; occasionally the waves, especially after a spell of warmish weather, will deposit brownish flakes of foam on the beach. This foam will probably consist of minute particles of sand and diatoms and even if there are no jars handy a blob of the foam placed on a piece of paper will leave, after a few minutes, a damp, brown-coloured patch; if the paper is placed in an envelope for safety the diatoms will survive the journey home.

In the section on Plankton the various other collecting methods are dealt with more fully. In any case it will be seen that there should be little difficulty in obtaining sufficient material to occupy many hours with the microscope without having to purchase slides. 'Type' slides, of course, are very useful in the, sometimes, difficult matter of identifying the different species of which some 13,000 are so far known.

The diatom itself consists of two halves which fit, one over the other, like a pill-box and its lid. Where the two halves overlap there is a 'girdle', known as the raphe. The shape of the different families varies considerably, as do their habits. *Bacillaria paradoxa*, for example, looks like a raft of logs and it is by no means unusual to find forty or more individuals thus placed side by side. A curious feature of this very common species (it is particularly common in off-shore waters and in estuaries as well as fresh water) is the manner in which it moves. As you look at the colony, first one 'log' will advance and then another so that the general shape of the raft is for ever changing.

Some species are found in strings, either joined at the corners, at the ends or, in the case of the circular kinds, on top of each other like a stack of plates. Other colonial forms exhibit a fan-like structure. Many of the solitary kind are boat shaped, others are like needles pointed at both ends whilst some resemble minute pill-boxes.

But apart from the diatom itself as an organism, the microscopist has found it to be a valuable test for the quality of the lenses. Many diatoms are perforated by a number of dots which are arranged differently according to the species. Some of these will be in lines running more or less parallel with the outline, some cross it diagonally, some in many weird geometrical designs, sculpturings and arabesques. Ordinarily, with medium-powers or mediocre lenses (or badly arranged illumination) these infinitely minute dots look like lines, but a good lens of sufficient power should be able to resolve these lines into their component dots.

The microscopists of the latter half of the last century were so keen on resolving these dots that the opticians were at their wits' end to supply ever better lenses, thus it was that these students, who were satirically called 'diatomaniacs', were responsible in great measure for the excellence of present-day lenses.

Apart, however, from the 'dot spotters' there was, and still is, a great army of people who, like myself, consider the diatom as being one of the most beautiful of all living things, and the most exasperating. There is, too, no little sense of achievement in successfully separating the diatoms from the unwanted matter and making a neat, workmanlike mount of them.

They may be mounted either in glycerine jelly, Canada balsam or as a dry mount. For details of all three techniques see the chapter on 'Mounting'.

FORAMINIFERA

Just as diatoms are the smallest plants, so the foraminifera are the smallest animals—with the exception of some of the flagellates and bacteria. Like the diatom it has a hard shell, either perforated with a number of tiny holes or with one or more 'foramina' or larger openings through which the jelly-like, single-celled animal protrudes itself in search of food. It is, in reality, an amoeba in a suit of chalky armour. This may have a definite chalk-like look or it may have a glassy appearance; on the other hand it may consist of a number of grains of sand cemented together in the semblance of a design. Ordinarily the shape is clear-cut and dainty, taking the form of a vase, star, spiral, disc or a host of other designs; the size, as a rule, is that of a grain of sand.

They are most prolific in the sea where they live amid the bustle of the tides and waves. Certain species inhabit fresh water and also estuaries, but their numbers and the variety of species are far fewer than in the sea. Their life is a short one and when they die the empty shells fall gradually to the bottom where, in some parts of the ocean bed, they form layers of fine silt many feet in thickness. Deep-sea dredges and sounding machines bring samples containing foraminifera to the surface. From the nature of these soundings the fog-bound mariner can get some idea of his position.

Many millions of years ago shells of these fragile little animals lived in the seas adjacent to this country, when one day the sea-bed arose exposing the silt to the air. The action of the air on the calcareous silt caused it to set hard in time, the resultant 'rock' becoming chalk. Therefore, all else failing, the enthusiast can turn to a piece of chalk for microscope fodder.

Plate VIII

DIATOMS

1. *Cymatopleura elliptica.*
2. *Achnanthes brevipes.*
3. *Pleurosigma formosum.*
4. *Amphiprora alata.*
5. *Triceratium favus.*
6. *Gomphonema capitatum.*
7. *Navicula amphisbaena.*
8. *Pinnularia major.*
9. *Amphora ovalis.*
10. *Encyonema prostratum.*
11. *Campylodiscus parvulus.*
12. *Melosira nummuloides.*
13. *Melosira arenaria.*
14. *Tryblionella gracilis.*
15. *Cocconeis scutellum.*
16. *Epithemia ventricosa.*
17. *Navicula rhomboides.*
18. *Eupodiscus argus.*

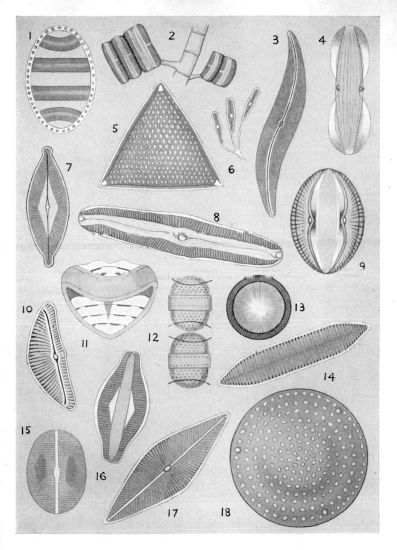

Plate VIII

Plate IX

PLATE IX

FRESHWATER FORMS OF THE
LOWER ANIMALS

1. Amoeba. Usually found amongst the confervae and duckweed on the surface of the pond.
2. *Clathrulina elegans*. This elegant Radoliarian may be found on the rootlets and undersides of the leaves of duckweed in shady pools and is more likely to be found in Ireland or Wales.
3. *Chaetonotus acanthomorphas*. The Gastrotrichas are also known as 'bristle backs'. Although they live in great numbers amongst the weeds and debris of the bottom with some of the rotifers they are often overlooked because of their small size. The very largest is only about 1/20" in length.
4. *Actinosphaericum Eichornii*. This protozoan may be found near the surface of ponds amongst the duck-weeds. It has the power of encysting itself in a siliceous coat in winter.
5. Green Hydra (*Chlorohydra viridissima*). Ordinarily this freshwater 'jellyfish' may be found adhering to plants and stones or hanging from the surface film of ponds. When fully extended the length may be half an inch.
6. Water Bear (*Tardigrada*). One of the great mysteries of the animal world—it bears no relationship whatever to any other group, moreover it is found throughout the world from the North Pole to the South.
7. *Ethmolaimus americanus*, a Nematode.
8. *Planaria gonocephala*, one of the Flatworms. It crawls over stones and plant stems or swims freely about in the water of the pond.
9. Bryozoa colony. *Cristatella mucedo* (after Allman). One of the Moss Animalcules.
10. Bryozoa. *Paludicella articulata*.
11. Bryozoa. *Fredericella sultana*.

The Bryozoa prefer submerged tree roots or the piles of old landing-stages in fairly deep water. Some colonies have a gelatinous appearance and superficially resemble clusters of eggs of water snails.

Unfortunately, it is not all chalks that will yield up the elusive 'foram' (as they are called for short); school chalk, for example, has been treated by machinery to render it smooth, and in the process the forams have been crushed out of all semblance to their original shapes. The same applies, even, to chalk taken from certain localities, ceaseless pressure for countless years has smashed many of the more delicate types, probably; on the other hand, the chalk may be of a kind formed by materials other than those supplied by the foraminifera; finally, an unsatisfactory method of handling the material will lead to failure.

Nearly every household has, stowed away somewhere or other, pieces of chalk brought home as souvenirs of South Coast holidays, and these pieces may prove rich in material. There are two ways of finding this out: the piece may be brushed lightly with an old tooth brush, under water, and the soft, white mud so produced examined under the microscope. The brushing has to be done lightly otherwise the more fragile shells will be crushed.

The other way is really more satisfactory in many respects, particularly if there is a fair amount of chalk on hand. Break the chalk up into lumps about the size of a walnut and place them in a piece of muslin of a convenient size, using not more than half a pound of chalk lumps at a time. Draw the ends of the muslin together and tie a piece of string round the material just above the chalk, just as though you were going to make plum duff. Immerse the bag so formed in a bowl of water for a day or two then, as the chalk softens, the minute particles will ooze through the muslin. It will take some time before the whole mass is softened and it may require a little assistance, this consisting of gently kneading the mass with the fingers. Some of the particles that ooze through may be very tiny forams so it is well to examine the fine mud that settles on the bottom of the bowl. Change the water frequently until all that is eventually left in the muslin is the insoluble matter; this may consist of tiny pieces of flint, sponge and *Alcyonium* spicules and forams; perhaps! Nevertheless, with patience, success will crown one's efforts.

Also it must be remembered that most of the chalk forams will be chalky-white in colour and at first glance will look like nothing other than a fragment of chalk, especially those with an irregular shape. Consequently, when examining chalk material either for spicules or forams it is advisable to try top light as well as reflected light.

The treatment of material containing living,

or recent, specimens is slightly different. Sometimes, for instance, a particular part of the beach, where the tide leaves ripple marks, is a good hunting ground; considerable quantities can be scraped up with a spoon. Mud exposed at low water, if its surface is scraped, may yield a fair gathering, and the same applies to the mud and sand at the lake side.

Whatever method of collecting is used the gatherings will all require the same treatment to separate the forams from the sand and other unwanted materials. (Incidentally, I should mention that they are also found in plankton collections, but the treatment will be the same.) The gathering should be spread out on a sheet of paper to dry and then when thoroughly dry tipped into a shallow bowl of water. The forams, owing to the fact that their insides will be hollow and filled with air (owing to the jelly-like part being dried up), will be buoyant; as a result, the sand will sink to the bottom leaving our specimens floating on the surface and all that has to be done is to remove them.

At least, that is the theory of it; in practice several outsize snags crop up as they usually do in microscope work, especially when a method has the virtue of being a simple one.

Many of the smaller specimens do not float and

so sink to the bottom with the sand; these have to be sought out separately and picked up in the manner as described for picking out desmids. Fortunately, even the smallest foram is larger and less fragile than any of the desmids. Then, for those that float, we are faced with the comparatively easy task of removing them from the surface of the water. This can be a rather tedious proceeding particularly if the gathering is a rich one. A soft paint brush will certainly pick them up, a dozen or more at a time, but it is most reluctant to part with its cargo; the only way seems to be that of having a small jar of water close by, or a specimen tube in which the catch can be stored, and dabbing the loaded brush therein. Even then the brush will only give up part of its load.

A better way is to have a number of small pieces of filter or blotting paper each about one and a half inches square and to draw them, one at a time, over the surface of the water. Each will pick up its own small quota of forams; then when the surface has been swept clean of all its floating forams, the blotting papers can be dried and their cargoes either tapped on to a slide for immediate examination and mounting or into a small specimen tube for preservation until we are ready to deal with them.

Foraminifera may be mounted dry, as a fluid

mount, or in glycerine jelly, Canada balsam, etc. If they are to be preserved in fluid do not use formalin, as the acid will eventually dissolve the chalky shells. In this way at least one valuable collection from the far ends of the earth has arrived at the Natural History museum as little more than a heap of mud. Alcohol, glycerine and water or camphor and distilled water are the best liquids for this purpose. Nevertheless, I have found the most convenient way is to preserve them dry.

So far so good. The next thing is to discuss the best ways of seeing the little shells under the microscope. Here we encounter some slight difficulty. The larger specimens, and some of the smaller ones, too, are more or less opaque and reflected light is a hindrance rather than a help. The transparent or semi-transparent kinds are probably seen at their best with reflected light but both kinds should be viewed with top light as well.

Some species look very different when seen from different angles and so, to get an all-round picture it is best to examine them on the point of a needle. If the point is lightly dipped in gum the specimen will be held securely enough whilst the needle is rotated slowly under the lens. If there is a pair of stage forceps with our outfit this operation can be carried out much more efficiently and easily. The needle will be held steady in the forceps which, in this case, will be rotated.

Some species are very delicately constructed indeed and one wonders how they could possibly have survived the rough and tumble of the waves. Others are quite robust and are more or less opaque. The latter, usually, are chambered and to see the design of these chambers more clearly sections should be made from different angles, one across the face of the specimen, one at right-angles, and the other diagonally. I admit that at first thought this appears to be a most formidable task; nevertheless, one gains a certain familiarity in handling these tiny shells after a time and a lightness of touch is acquired.

The best way of making these sections is to take, first, two wooden matchsticks and apply a thin smear of spirit gum to the end of each match opposite the head. Then lightly touch the specimen with the gummed end of one of the matches, to which it will adhere. Regard it with a magnifying glass or with a very low-power under the microscope and adjust it to the desired position with a needle. Now take a slip of Washita, India or other similar smooth abrasive stone and draw it very lightly across the face of the specimen at right angles to the matchstick. So small and so delicate are most specimens that the one operation is usually sufficient to grind the surface away. However, it should be carefully examined under the glass to make sure that enough has been removed. Apply a drop of spirit to the match-end, this will dissolve the gum, so that, when the gummed end of the other match is applied to the foram it will adhere to that, the unground face uppermost. The stone, lightly applied as before, should leave a thin section sticking to the match. Have a glass slip handy, its centre slightly smeared with gum; a drop of spirit will release the section so that when the slip is touched with the match-end the section will be transferred to it ready for mounting. The microscope will now reveal the intricate inner structure on which the identification of many species depends. The ideal mount should consist of the same species mounted at different angles and with two or more sections made from different angles.

Foraminifera, like diatoms, are essentially a study for the microscope enthusiast and a most satisfying study they make indeed; there is the thrill in searching for them, taking one out into the open air; the satisfaction of making a scientific study of the group; the skill that is demanded from hand, eye and mind, and on top of all there is the undoubted beauty, available to tyro and expert alike.

CHAPTER VII

MARINE MICROSCOPY

THE seas provide a prodigious wealth of microscope material, often where we least expect it.
To most of us the seashore will be the limit of our
marine explorations and before we go any further,
lest the reader who does not live near the sea turns
regretfully away from this chapter without read-
ing on, let me hasten to describe what I call my
'quick, sharp and handy' method of collecting on
the seashore and thereabouts. It is a method that
can be adopted with profit even if one can only
get to the coast on a day excursion.

Naturally, such an excursion is planned at the
onset as a day out and may be made in the company of a lot of other people; as such it is not
designed to cope with an armoury of collecting
equipment. Nevertheless, even if only a couple of
small stoppered bottles can be slipped into the
pocket or handbag sufficient material could be
collected to provide many hours of pleasant
microscope browsing and the ensuing mounting
of objects for the cabinet.

A scraping of the surface mud of a beach such as that at Southend-on-Sea, a clump of the bright green weed that festoons out when the tide is in and which hangs limp and damp when it is out (mostly found growing from the piles of piers, groynes and stones), both will provide material, each in its different way. The weed, although it may have been abandoned by the tide for several hours, will house diatoms, copepods and occasional foraminifera amongst other things. The mud scrapings will contain different species of those same organisms. Even if the beach is of hard sand scrapings from beneath stones, shells or from sheltered hollows should produce some useful material.

The scrapings should be put into one of the jars with some sea water, although the latter is not an essential. Unless the idea is to study the living organisms, formalin should be added straightaway, for some of the more delicate kinds will rapidly decompose, especially during the course of a long and hot train journey. The fine weed may also be rammed into a jar and, if so desired, formalin added.

If the shore is very rocky or is one where the larger sea-weeds pile up on the tide line, a clump of the weed can be rewarding if wrapped up in a newspaper and then washed in a large measuring glass or beaker of fresh water when you get home. The organisms will fall to the bottom of the glass and can then be easily removed to other quarters with the pipette. The fronds themselves should be carefully examined for clinging crustaceans and for patches of Flustra, otherwise known as the 'Sea mat', a close relation of the Bryozoa of the fresh water. In this case the colony consists of individuals which form a calcareous shell round themselves and so it has a chalky appearance.

In tidal pools look particularly for molluscs— or their empty shells—for on their inner surface you may find the eggs of various marine creatures whilst the outside of the shell may support barnacles, apart from other larger organisms. Barnacles are also to be found on rocks and stones and, in fact, on almost any stationary or slow-moving object. The barnacle makes a most attractive preparation. First remove it from its anchorage with a sharp knife and then with a pair of tweezers extract the animal. Place it in a watch-glass of water and add a drop of formalin; gently tease out the appendages which will soon fan out in the liquid. Mount as a fluid mount in a cell and you will find that with top light or as a polarizer subject it provides a most delightful preparation.

But to continue with our other material; the

lucky collector may find when the tide is really low some of the encrusting sponges and other growths on solid objects such as the piles of piers and landing-stages, these house isopods, amphipods and other small sea creatures of retiring habit.

I admit that the collecting hints I have given are more applicable to those who are fortunate enough to spend a week or more beside the briny. Still, one or more of the methods described should reasonably be possible even for a very short visit.

Now for the handling of the material after it has been grabbed, snatched or scraped from its habitat. The clumps of weed and the attendant moisture are placed in a beaker of fresh water and the weed well washed in it. The fresh water kills the organisms which lurk in the shelter of the weed or cling to its fronds; they will then settle on the bottom of the beaker from which they can be removed in the approved manner—with a pipette, transferred to a specimen tube of suitable size, formalin added to a strength of 3% and put away for future reference.

The mud and sand collection presents a different problem altogether because there are several different kinds of organisms present with the necessarily different techniques of extraction; diatoms, foraminifera and copepods. My own method is to examine a fairly thick solution spread on a glass slip and remove the larger organisms with pipette to a watch-glass of water and divide the remainder into two halves, decanting one half for diatoms and treating the other half for foraminifera as described in the preceding chapter.

Sometimes it is not necessary to travel as far as the sea for marine specimens. If we can obtain ungutted herrings from the fishmonger we should be able to add some planktonic organisms to our collection, for the herring feeds entirely on plankton—of which more anon. Cut open the abdomen (I have found sharp-pointed scissors the most efficient implement for this job) and remove the stomach, placing it in a vessel containing a 2% formalin solution—this arrests any further decomposition, of which quite sufficient has already been going on. Well stir the contents and transfer a small portion to a glass slide. A great part will consist of semi-digested and decomposed matter, giving a cloudy appearance to the fluid, but here and there will be copepods, some of which may be entire, and other organisms. The diatoms, because of their hard shell are usually found in a more or less undamaged condition. Foraminifera, likewise, have been found in herring stomachs, also certain of the really tiny plankton organisms that require very high powers before they will condescend to reveal their construction. Of these the most likely to survive a sojourn in the interior of a fish are the dinoflagellates of which more will be said later. Herring stomachs are indeed a happy hunting ground for the microscopist and, even though one may draw blank at times, the majority will more than pay for the initial outlay in purchasing the fish, which, in any case, can be eaten.

Not many of the fish displayed on the fish-monger's slab are plankton feeders. Cod, hake and the other large fishes prefer a more robust diet; flat fishes, such as the sole and plaice, feed on worms and young shell-fish; whitebait, how-ever, feed on the plankton and so does the smelt to a certain degree. The shad feeds partially on the plankton but, strangely enough, the sprat that is offered for sale during the winter months will be found to have a comparatively empty stomach although it is a vegetable feeder. The answer to this is that the sprat does most of its feeding in the summer. Grey mullet are an excellent source, especially in the matter of brackish-water dia-toms; they feed by literally sucking with their leathery lips the diatoms that adhere to the grass-like weed already referred to, and which grows on stones and wooden staging. It also sucks small organisms from the mud. Unfortunately it is not often that one comes across this very tasty but elusive fish.

Certain molluscs such as the oyster, cockle and mussel feed on the very minute things by drawing them into the stomach by producing a current of water. The method of emptying the very small stomachs demands a good knowledge of the molluscan anatomy so I do not intend to enlarge on it other than by saying a pipette drawn to a fine point is inserted in the mouth region and another in the anus and a stream of water poured into the former; the stomach contents then pass along the second pipette and are collected in a beaker. A very tedious business altogether but most rewarding as one often finds the really tiny diatoms that elude even the fine meshed plankton net.

There is one more aspect of marine creatures that must not be overlooked and that is the construction of the tongue or radula of certain of the molluscs, especially the whelks, limpets and winkles. The tongue is used by these creatures to rasp their food (algae and the like) from weeds, rocks and stones. If we watch a snail in the aquarium browsing on the green algae that forms on the glass we shall be able to see how it does this. We shall also be able to see exactly where to look for the tongue itself, for usually it is very tiny

PLATE X

MINUTE CRUSTACEA

1. *Cyclops demetiensis.* 2mm. Freshwater Copepod.
2. *Canthocamptus furcatus.* 0.5mm. Freshwater Copepod.
3. *Diaptomus castor.* 2mm. Freshwater Copepod.
4. *Canthocamptus staphylinus.* 0.5mm. Freshwater Copepod.
5. *Cyclops phaleratus.* 2mm. Freshwater Copepod.
6. *Cypris vidua.* Species of Ostracod. Freshwater.
7. *Cyclops quadricornis* (*nauplius*, 8 days old). Freshwater Copepod.
8. *Cypris monarcha.* Species of Ostracod. Freshwater.
9. *Pontellina.* Copepod. Marine plankton.
10. *Polyphemus pediculus.* 2mm. Freshwater Cladocera.
11. *Calocalanus pavo.* Copepod. Oceanic plankton.
12. *Candace ethiopica.* Copepod. Marine plankton.

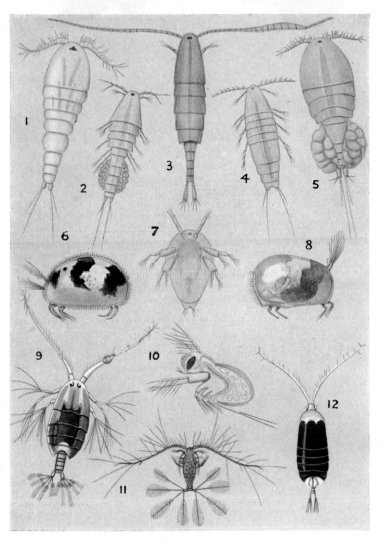

Plate X

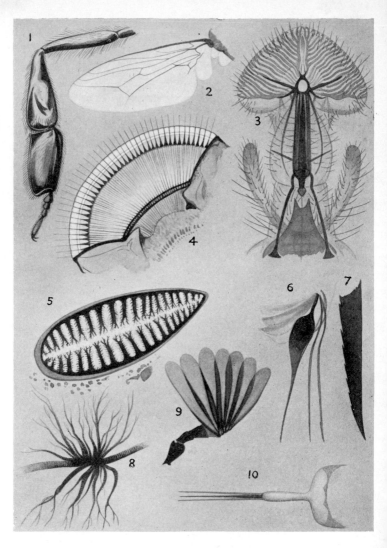

Plate XI

PLATE XI

DISSECTIONS OF INSECTS

1. Leg of Bee.
2. Wing of Tsetse Fly.
3. Proboscis of Blow Fly.
4. Section through eye of Butterfly.
5. Spiracle of Water Beetle.
6. Sting of Bee.
7. Point of sting highly magnified.
8. Trachea of Blow Fly.
9. Antenna of Cockchafer.
10. Ovipostor of Wood Wasp.

although often, relatively, of considerable length. It consists of a horny ribbon covered with rows of minute teeth. No two species seem to have the same kind of tongue, though; some have hundreds of tiny teeth, others have fewer and larger ones; in some they are four deep, in others five, six or even more deep.

They are not always easy to find for they lie curled up behind the mouth, a little piece of the end being thrust out to collect the food. If we find the mouth first, then the matter is not quite so difficult. Place the mollusc first of all in some alcohol to kill it (and also preserve until we are ready to deal with it) and then in a small trough of water the dissecting operation can commence. The necessary implements are a mounted needle, a pair of sharp-pointed scissors and forceps with thin, slightly in-curved ends. With the scissors the object is cut open at the mouth region, then with the needle the tissues are explored for the thin ribbon which may have a length when straightened out of a quarter of an inch or more. When it has been located it should be removed and placed in water for a few days to remove unwanted tissue and any other extraneous matter. Now the radula of these molluscs make a delightful preparation for the polarizer and for this purpose they should be placed on a glass slip and allowed to dry and a drop of Canada balsam dropped on them. Place in a warm place until all the air bubbles have come to the surface (these will be removed by pricking with a needle) and

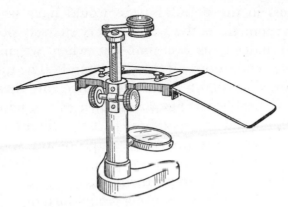

FIG. 11.—DISSECTING MICROSCOPE WITH ARM RESTS. VERY USEFUL FOR SUCH OPERATIONS AS REMOVING RADULAE

then cover with a cover-glass. Otherwise they may be mounted in glycerine jelly or as a fluid mount.

PLANKTON

Now for what, in my opinion, is the most interesting part of the marine scene so far as the microscopist is concerned—the plankton, that seething world of minute life occupying the upper layers of the water and on which nearly all sea creatures ultimately rely for their food. The larger organisms feed on the smaller and they in turn are devoured by still larger creatures, like Dean Swift's 'fleas' in reverse.

Not that the water is as full of plankton as writers in the popular press would have us believe; sometimes the water is very sparsely populated indeed, as we find out when we make regular collections all the year round. The ultra-microscopic plant forms, of course, are nearly always prolific. They are known as the nannoplankton and their study is particularly difficult. Indeed, the very first monograph of any weight on the subject is only very recently published. I will say no more about them other than that you will notice them when using a one-third or higher power objective on living material as more or less oval bodies, semi-transparent, oozing their way around the other plankton material on the slide. The colour may be pale green, yellowish or brownish-green or orange.

The most usual way of obtaining a 'sample' is to tow a plankton net behind a boat with the net working at about six feet (or more, according to the depth of water) below the surface. It is a similar net to that described in the chapter on Pond Life Microscopy for obtaining plankton from lakes. The Apstein type of plankton net as used in marine work is made from bolting silk of the kind used in flour milling and having sixty meshes to the linear inch. This is considered as being a rather 'coarse' net but it is ideal for capturing copepods or other organisms of a similar size as well as smaller fry. For the even smaller material the silk should have 180 meshes to the inch.

A plastic 'bucket' is attached to the end of the net at its apex and this, by means of a bayonet attachment, can be removed after the net has been hauled in after its trawl. The catch can then be tipped into a glass jar for transportation.

Naturally, it is not always possible to obtain the services of a boat owner, nor can we spare the time entailed by a trip in a boat. But that need not necessarily deter us. In most seaside towns there is a pier past which the water flows with the tides. If the pier is situated similarly to the one at Southend-on-Sea the tide will flow fairly strongly (at about four knots) and this is quite sufficient to 'fish' the net efficiently. The method I adopt, in order to keep the net level at the right depth, is to have three cords fixed equidistant on the part the bucket fits into and at the end of these cords I tie a lead weight. Also, at about two yards from the mouth of the net I tie another weight to the tow-rope.

A quarter of an hour should suffice to accumulate a reasonable quantity of plankton, provided the tide is 'fishing' the net properly.

If one's resources cannot run to either owning or hiring a boat, or if there is no convenient pier, or even if one does not possess a net, there is no need to give up in despair. Microscopists are nothing if not resourceful; here is a method I used for quite a long time for obtaining inshore plankton samples. I obtained a cylindrical tin (the exact size is really immaterial) about a foot tall and seven inches in diameter. With a tin opener and much perseverance, I cut the bottom out, thus leaving a cylinder open at both ends. The next proceeding was to obtain some muslin, not a very difficult feat, and to cut out some discs having a diameter somewhat greater than that of the tin. Bolting silk, of course, is much to be preferred because the plankton is apt to adhere to the muslin and is difficult to wash out. However, a disc of the material was tied tightly over one end of the tin—just as it is tied over the end of the Apstein's bucket; then, with an ordinary dipper or pail, a length of rope and the contraption just described I set out for the nearest groyne, breakwater, jetty or projecting rocks. The bucket was lowered into the water, hauled up, and the contents poured into the cylinder. The water filtered through the material quite quickly and the performance was repeated a dozen times or more, according to the degree of my tiredness or the size of the crowd that sometimes collected to watch and ask silly questions.

I need hardly remark that it is not a good idea to wear your best clothes for this job, in fact shorts or a bathing costume are the ideal wear except in the cold weather.

Well, here we are with our jar containing the catch plus a reasonable quantity of sea water. To kill and preserve the catch formalin should be added, making a 3% solution. The next thing is to make a rough examination of the material, and the best way of doing this, I have found, is to tip it all into a very large petri dish or some similar type of glassware, even if you have to borrow it from the kitchen. At the side of the dish there should be a watch-glass or similar object in which is a weak formalin solution. We shall also require some tweezers, a few glass slips, a pipette (not with too fine a nozzle) and the microscope.

Some of the organisms will be relatively large, up to half an inch in length, perhaps. In this category will be mysids, worms such as *sagitta* and *tomopteris*, *amphipods*, baby shrimps and fishes, jelly-fishes, *isopods*, *cumacea*, *cladocera*. These should be removed and transferred to the watch-glass to be examined and mounted later—as a fluid mount in a cell, for preference, or in glycerine jelly.

The smaller objects will not now be masked by their larger companions. Take up some of them in a pipette and deposit on a glass slip, taking

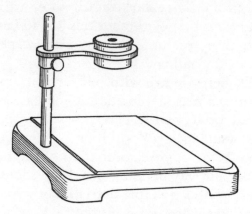

FIG. 12.—ANOTHER TYPE OF DISSECTING MICRO-
SCOPE, USEFUL FOR SORTING OUT THE LARGE
PLANKTON TYPES

care that there is not too much fluid and also that the stage is level. It is very annoying to find the material slowly wandering away just when you have come across something of an especially interesting nature. It is a good idea to leave it for some minutes, until the objects have settled, and then tip the slide and let the water drip off one of the corners. But it is good to see that the stage is perfectly dry; it is so easy for some of the fluid to get on it and this makes the slip difficult to manipulate.

When you are finally all set, start at one end of the slip, gripping it at the corners (unless there is a mechanical stage) and work in a straight line from top to bottom, then move it along a little and repeat the operation. In this way all the objects on the slip will have been observed. There are bound to be some objects that we should like to mount at once. If we have had this in mind then the glycerine jelly will already be standing in some hot water and we can make the preparation straightaway. In any case, the various methods of picking out the organisms we wish to mount are dealt with elsewhere as well as the mounting details.

After all our bother, hard work and battles with the elements, what are we likely to find for our pains?

Well, there will be the diatoms, many of which will differ considerably from those of the fresh water. For the most part they will be more robust and many will belong to different families. The accompanying plate shows some of the species likely to be found in the littoral waters of the British Isles.

In estuaries, where the tides scour the sea-bed, one is almost bound to find foraminifera both in the living and dead state. Do not leave them in the formalin if you wish to preserve them. If only particular specimens are required these can be removed individually from the glass slip. But if as many as possible are to be salvaged they can be extracted from the sample after it has been thoroughly explored by the method given in the section devoted to foraminifera.

Next we come to *Noctiluca*, one of the Cyto-flagellates. A fascinating little creature, this, and one that always reminds me of a nasturtium leaf, stalk included. At times the water will be full of them and when this happens we are treated at night, usually, to a fine display of phosphorescence on the surface. When there are any in the catch the water in the jar will appear to be full of small floating particles. It is a diatom feeder and, so transparent is this tiny creature, the diatoms which it has recently engulfed can be seen quite clearly in its interior; *Paralia sulcata* and *Melosira* being very popular with *Noctiluca*. In August and September, when it is most prolific in the Thames Estuary, the diatom *Rhizosolenia stolter-fothii* may be noticed as having recently engaged its attentions.

Next we come to the Dinoflagellates, represented principally in the catch of the finer net. The most commonly encountered kind is that known as *Tintinnopsis*, the Bell Ciliate. There are many species of this in our waters but nearly all of them have a bell-like appearance, or that of the sort of thimble the smallest of all fairies would wear.

The catch, especially from May to August, may present a strange appearance, almost as though it has turned into a thin jelly. This will have been caused by a flagellate known as *Phaeocystis* to the biologist and 'bacca juice' by the fisherman. It clogs his nets and gives a distinct unpleasant odour to the water and, from its jelly-like structure, will even fill his nets with useless matter to the exclusion of his legitimate catch. The flagellate responsible has the unpleasant habit of forming this jelly round itself. The microscopist, unfortunately, will not find it of any great interest, it is so tiny and difficult to see properly. It is here mentioned because the plankton student will come across it sooner or later and may wonder what it is all about.

Amongst the slightly larger organisms there will be the small jellyfishes, the Antho-, Lepto- and Discomedusae. They form delightful microscope objects whilst they are alive and for a few weeks after being preserved. The colours often are delightful and so are the shapes. They never attain anything like the size of the jellyfishes that we find stranded on the beach (these are, for the most part, Discomedusae) and, as a rule, arise from the sea-weed-like Zoophytes, close relations of the 'White weed' now so popular when dyed for table decorations. By far the best way of making preparations of them is to mount them in fluid, by any other means there is great risk of distortion.

Two stages in the development of the little star-fishes will be seen, and very attractive they are too, especially when seen by top light or with the polarizer. These stages are known as the Bipinnaria and the Echinopluteus stages. They may be mounted by any of the ordinary methods. The related *Alcyonium*, although of rare occurrence in its young stages is represented by the cast-off spicules of the adult. The spicules of other lowly creatures may be found in plankton where the bottom of the sea has been stirred up by the tides —especially of sponges and *Gorgonia*. These make delightful polarizer material.

In the larger material (known as the macro-plankton) we are almost bound to find specimens of that interesting worm, *Sagitta*, of which two species are found in British waters. It has a length of half an inch or so and is a pale greenish-blue colour. It does not resemble the popular conception of a worm except in its attenuated shape.

There are fish-like fins towards the tail end, and at the end of the tail itself there is a typical caudal fin. Moreover, it is not segmented and is almost transparent. It is best mounted in glycerine jelly (in which it goes yellowish in time) or as a fluid mount.

Nearly, but not all, of the worms of the sea-bed, such as the lugworm and ragworm and numerous other species spend their early days in the surface waters. Their nectosome and post-larval stages are frequently represented. Some of the poly-chaetes are purely planktonic and spend all their lives amongst the waves. Of these there are to be found *Autolytus* and *Tomoptera*. They should be mounted in the same manner as *Sagitta*.

Of the crustacea, first should be mentioned the barnacle, several species of which infest the bottoms of ships and the piles of piers, etc. The cast-off skins of adults are often seen in inshore samples; the preparing of these for examination is more or less the same as for the adults already described. Just as interesting are the various stages, and they are many, of the transition from the egg, through the nauplius stages to the 'cypris' stage before it finally settles down to a sedentary existence as an adult. It may be mounted in fluid or in jelly or Canada balsam.

Almost certainly there will be one or other of

the many species of copepod, the most common of which in inshore waters is *Acartia clausi*, closely followed by *Temora longicornis*. Harpacticids also will be represented and most certainly if they are present *Euterpina acutifrons* will be there.

The Cladocera, so well known to the pond life enthusiast in the form of daphnia, are not very well represented in the sea. A few species of the families Podon and Evadne inhabit the North Sea and elsewhere but they are rare in inshore waters.

The Amphipoda, relations of the larger fresh water flea, *Gammarus pulex*, may be found in the macro-plankton. Where there is any weed we are almost certain to find that weird little creature, the ghost shrimp. Although not exactly 'microscopic' they make interesting fluid mounts for use with the lower powers.

The Cumacea, especially the species *Pseudocuma similis*, are common to inshore waters. In deeper water and further from the land there are numerous other species frequently found.

The Mysids, close relations of the 'krill' on which the Right Whales feed, have one very common species especially in inshore waters; this is *Macropsis slabberi* which has an average length of eleven millimetres. They are very shrimp-like in appearance and must form a valuable addition to the diet of the fishes.

Very small adult shrimps sometimes find their way into the catch but it is a strange thing that the larger organisms seem to be forced out of the net by the force of the water. Baby shrimps will be found as well as larval crabs, and larval crabs are very funny-looking things indeed, and no one would ever guess that they would finish up as they do. The spines that stick out right in front of the head and behind the tail will stretch over quite a large part of the slide. Both the baby shrimps and the baby crabs as well as most of the tiny crustaceans make good fluid mounts.

A very interesting object will present itself to the view of the microscopist who is examining plankton from inshore waters. It will look something like a saucer and be about the same size as *Noctiluca*; that is to say, visible as a small mote in the water. It will be semi-transparent except for the central part and the colour a very pale greenish-blue. This is the egg of the Common Winkle and at times it is very plentiful indeed and may be found in nearly every month of the year, thus showing that the winkle has a most protracted breeding season. Baby cockles and other bivalve molluscs, looking very much like their parents, are also to be seen as well as the very young stages.

Oikopleura dioica and its relatives often prove

very puzzling when first seen. They have thin bodies and a large head and look just like tadpoles. They are the adults of an animal that never grows up, the Appendicularian, a relative of the Sea Squirt, the young of which also is a 'tadpole' and inhabits the plankton, too. The adult may be found on rocks and pieces of timber looking like a colourful limpet with the body covering looking soft and leathery. The most interesting point about the Sea Squirts or Tunicates, to give them their correct name, is that they are without any sort of 'backbone' whatever in the adult state yet their larvae have a threadlike and very primitive form of backbone. *Oikopleura* has a notochord, as this kind of backbone is called, throughout their lives.

Baby fishes are always interesting, especially when a Schultz preparation has been made (see section on 'Mounting'). Particularly noticeable are the chromatophores or colour-cells which, instead of being spread evenly over the body as they are in the adult fish, are grouped irregularly in comparatively large patches. The fins, too, stand out clearly and the eyes can be really delightful. In the very small fry the backbone can be clearly seen with strong reflected light but in time the muscle tissue becomes more or less opaque. Many species of fife when in the larval stage do not in the least resemble their parents; in our own waters this is especially the case with the so-called flatfishes. In them the eyes are set on each side of the head, whereas in the adult they are both on the same side. They may be mounted either in fluid, glycerine jelly or Canada balsam.

The eggs of fishes also should be found in the plankton. The identification of these is a difficult affair altogether and it generally depends on whether there are oil globules present and if so on whether they are large or small. The diameter also plays a big part in running them to earth as well as the time of the year in which they were captured. A fluid mount always seems to me to be the best way to mount them.

NOTE.—To prepare the cirri of *Balanus* or other similar kinds of barnacle the entire animal should be killed in formalin 10%. Then the body should be removed and the cirri separated from it and placed in 25% glycerine to allow the gases to escape. They may then be mounted as a fluid mount.

An attractive preparation of *Sagitta* and other chaetognaths can be made by staining deeply with Thionin and differentiating with acid alcohol to the required stage. This results in the body of the animal being blue and the fins pink.

CHAPTER VIII

GARDEN AND HEDGEROW

THERE is really very little difference in the type of material of a microscopic nature that the garden provides and that of the countryside. In a well-matured garden of any size a goodly number of wild organisms may often be found and so, even though we live in the heart of the city and a trip into the country would be a major operation, we can still find plenty to occupy the stage of the microscope. On the other hand, we may live so deep in the heart of the city that there is no garden attached to our house or flat—and a visit to the country may still be every bit as much of a major operation. Even so, there is no need to despair. There may be rusts and moulds on some of the greengrocer's stock, whilst many a butterfly and moth are attracted to houses, as are spiders and flies and the 'silver fish' of the pantry. Mosses grow in the crevices of brickwork and there are also the public parks.

At this point I must do some qualifying. The fact that you are an earnest seeker after know-

ledge will not make you any the more popular
with the authorities if you pick the flowers or dig
up plants by the roots. On the other hand, you
might quite possibly find a sympathetic park
superintendent who will let you have leaves, etc.,
with rust or mould on them, and any other interesting material that is of no use to any other
than the earnest seeker.

I will deal firstly, then, with the rusts and
moulds and assume that all my readers have
access both to the countryside and to a garden,
whether public or private.

On damp walls or on other solid objects in the
shade we may come across what looks like a large
patch of blood. This is known as 'Gory' Dew and
it belongs to a single-celled form of plant life. The
microscope will show it as consisting of a number
of single cells, usually contained in a gelatinous
envelope. Sometimes there may be as many as
sixteen such cells in the one container. The 'Red'
snow one hears about, is formed by several different species of a near relative, also of simple
construction, which causes considerable specula-
tion when it decides to tint the white surface of
the snow. The microscope soon reveals that it is a
single-celled plant.

The common mould, by the way, is a fungus. It
forms on jam and so forth and its name is *Peni-*

cillium glaucum, from which penicillin is made. The general pattern of this kind of fungus and its relatives, some of which are known as mildew, consists of a tangled mass of filaments not divided up into separate cells. From these filaments arise, at the appropriate time and under the right conditions, upright filaments with a ball at the end. This contains the spores and both the mycelium as the main mass of filaments is called and the sporangia will be differently coloured according to the species. Thus the mould that forms on bread and on leather goods left in the dark in a damp cupboard is of a pale, unpleasant green colour whilst the sporangia are black.

But do not think that because you have seen one type of mould, mildew or rust under the microscope you have seen them all. Apart from the differences in the colour there are great differences in the shape and design of the sporangia.

These fungi may be found as rust on wheat; most fruits, especially grapes, produce them. On the pea plant and the grape vine and on the leaves of many plants, especially in the autumn, mildews and rusts may be found. The last-named occur as brightly coloured patches in various shades of red and yellow and other colours as well as black. If some of the mould is scraped off and examined under a medium power their structure will be readily seen. In the case of fungi on leaves it is best to cut out a piece of the leaf with scissors to examine it. Many seeds also, to the gardener's disgust, develop mildew and when these are examined we can get a better view of the fungus because we can see the spores sticking out from the sides of the seeds.

In the autumn the Common Duck Weed (*Lemna minor*) presents us with a most unusual fungus, for this is found attached to the rootlets and also within the cells of the plant. The former take the form of projecting excrescences whilst the latter are thread-like as though the external form was the sporangium and the internal the mycelium.

Moving gradually up the plant life scale we come to the higher fungi, such as the common mushroom, which present many interesting features, especially if sections are cut from the fleshy part. Ferns, too, repay the attention of the low-powers, particularly the brown-coloured 'sori' which contain the spores. The spores themselves are contained within capsules and these make interesting preparations in their own right.

One of the most interesting collections, not only to prepare but also to collect, consists of the organs which bear the spores of the different species of moss. They are visible to the unaided eye but when magnified they are seen in their true beauty. The name given to the part of this organ which holds the spores is the 'urn' and it is capped with a curious little affair called the calyptra. If this is removed a conical body is revealed and when this is taken away numerous threads held together by tiny teeth will be seen; right in the centre are the spores. Cross-sections of these containers mounted in glycerine jelly make very attractive preparations.

A great variety of cells are revealed when we make sections of tissues from the fruit, leaves, stems and roots of the flowering plants. The leaves, and very often the petals, may be covered with 'hairs', many of which have unusual shapes. Many plants are hairy, the nettle in particular, but others are not obviously so, but the microscope will show that very often even if there are no hairs there will be protuberances, knobs, papillae and so forth covering the leaf. The hairs responsible for the sting in the nettle are transparent, so they should be removed from the leaf in their entirety and mounted dry; then their remarkable structure may be clearly observed.

In order to see the hairs on other leaves the usual instructions are to lift up a portion of the surface of the leaf and tear off a piece of the surface. This is generally easier said than done, for more often than not the thin epidermis has not the slightest intention of leaving the rest of the leaf. A good soak in water generally helps matters. Also on the surface of the leaf, principally on the underside, we can see the apertures through which the plant breathes. These are called stomata and they also have their attendant guard-cells which regulate the size of the stomata opening. To my mind there seems to be little point in making special preparations of these, even as fluid mounts, unless one is a serious botanist, and then the necessary and complicated techniques will be known to the student. Leaves are usually close at hand.

Cross-sections of the stems of such plants as the sunflower, nasturtium, delphinium, etc., are reasonably easy to prepare owing to the softish nature of the tissue. On the other hand, this very softness is often a drawback, for even the sharpest razor might distort the cellular structure. In this case the section of stem is placed in dilute alcohol for some hours to harden the tissue before the thin sections are made. Unfortunately, the alcohol will remove the colour. Then again stems of such plants as the rushes and water-lilies, and the leaves of the latter, are penetrated by air-cavities. So for these plants, and also if we wish to retain the colour, the subject is best embedded in gum.

We should make longitudinal as well as transverse sections of the stem for then the cells will be seen in a totally different aspect. With the aid of even an elementary textbook on botany the various parts may be identified—the cortex, epidermis, phloem, xylem, vascular bundles, pith, etc. Ordinarily the best fluid mount should be a weak alcohol one.

The anther cases of the flower's stamen are very interesting, especially if examined with a low-power just before they are ripe. The pollen will be seen, neatly tucked away, if the anther is cut through. An interesting collection of pollen slides can be made without any great bother—the thinnest of all possible smears of gum on the centre of a slide and the ripe anther tapped gently over it is all that is necessary. A ring of cement and a cover-glass pressed on to it and there is your mount. An amazing variety of designs are shown by the pollen grains of the different plants, far more than one could possibly imagine without having seen them. A cross-section through the ovary at the base of the pistil will reveal the seeds all ready to be fertilized by the pollen. The main design is readily visible to the unaided eye, of course, but nevertheless the microscope is necessary in order to see the beautiful sculpturing possessed by the testa (the thin membrane covering the seed), and to see this top light should be used. A section cut above the ovary might show the channels made by the pollen grains on their way to fertilize the seeds.

Finally, a word about the insects whose name is legion. Both town and countryside are well populated with insects that are either beautiful, interesting or a nuisance, very often all three.

The wings are always interesting. Many are covered with scales, those of the moths and butterflies being particularly obvious, but many of the inconspicuous insects also have scales. The *Podura* or Spring-tail, a metallic-looking little insect sometimes found on the brickwork of greenhouses and elsewhere, bears several different kinds of curiously marked scales. For years these scales have been used as a test of the quality of lenses. Then there is the so-called Silver Fish or *Lepsima* which is often found in the pantry; this also bears attractive scales. Incidentally, scales and wings should be mounted dry.

If the wings of many of the tiny insects are examined they will be found to be covered with long, spine-like hairs; they are quite interesting as a dry mount. In the fields at harvest time we are often made painfully aware of the attentions of the Harvest Mite and sometimes we may find one on the wheat stems as a tiny red dot. They are fearsome-looking creatures when magnified and have been mounted in glycerine jelly. Other tiny insects may be mounted either in that manner or dry.

The appendages of insects such as the bee require some preparation before they make a satisfactory preparation. They should be soaked in a 5% caustic potash solution for as long as a fortnight and then washed in clean water with a camel-hair brush. They are then placed between two glass slips held together by rubber bands and left in a warm place to dry. When they are thoroughly dry they are placed in turpentine until well soaked and mounted in Canada balsam in the usual way.

Ovipostors, stings and gizzards (such as the horny gizzard of the grasshopper and its kind) require considerable knowledge of the anatomy of insects generally if they are to be successfully dissected out.

The spiracles of such insects as the blowfly, bee, cockchafer and caterpillars generally, as well as the tracheae are not so difficult to dissect out. The spiracles lie on each side of the abdomen, each segment of which possesses a pair. Slit the abdomen down the middle with fine-pointed scissors and draw out the viscera. By cutting away the air tubes or tracheae the entire spiracles of both sides may be removed, well washed, dried between two slips, soaked in turpentine and mounted in balsam.

The tracheae removed in the foregoing operation, if in a good state, may be treated as were the spiracles. If they were not in a good state then another specimen must be selected and this time the spiracles will have to come off second best.

In dissecting organs from insects it is best, if the insect is of any size, to pin it to a thin piece of cork weighted with lead on the under-side and then place in a small trough of water. The water will wash away all the unwanted parts. If the abdomen is slit and then placed in strong acetic acid for a day the viscera will easily wash away. Attached to the stomach will be observed a small bulb. This should be cut open with the points of a fine-pointed pair of scissors and the mangled remains of the last meal removed. Wash the gizzard, for such this is, in water and press it out well and then place for a few days, to cleanse it thoroughly, in a weak solution of caustic potash. Then treat in the same manner as described for the spiracles, etc.

A formula for mounting tiny insects is given on page 203.

CHAPTER IX

MOUNTING MATERIALS AND APPLIANCES

WE have reviewed briefly a few of the many sources from which the microscopist can draw for material for examination. Many of the objects, either for their beauty or interest, will appeal to the student and the wish may arise to preserve them in such a way that they can be consulted at any future time.

There are a number of ways of achieving this and the method used will vary according to the subject or to any particular feature of the subject that is to be emphasized. The most favoured methods practised today fall into three rather diffusive groups, viz.:

(1) *Dry mounting*, in which the subject is in no preserving medium whatever. As a rule, by means of a thin film of gum, it is stuck to a glass slide and covered with a cover-glass.

(2) *Semi-dry mounting*, a method requiring a medium that can be used in a liquid state but will set hard or semi-hard afterwards. This is the most common method.

(3) *Fluid mounting*. This requires a slide to which a cell ring has been affixed or one that has an excavation. This method is of great value if all aspects of the subject are to be examined; floating, as it does in the fluid, first one and then another part faces the lens.

Sometimes, in order to gain as comprehensive a knowledge as possible, it is advisable to mount specimens of the same subject in various mediums. It is so easy to lose one's perspective when only one face of an object is examined or when it is seen under only one set of conditions.

No matter what method is used, however, there are two cardinal rules that must be observed if the mount is to be a success; they are, first, *absolute cleanliness* and, second, *system*.

It is possible, of course, to make microscope slides without observing either rule, but the results will be poor and the whole performance sloppy and slipshod. Microscope slide making can be one of the most delightful occupations possible and, in the long run, less expensive than many other hobbies. Moreover, there is a sense of achievement when a really workmanlike slide is made, comparable to that of the craftsman when he creates beautiful objects from uncouth materials.

Absolute cleanliness is not always easy to attain, try as you will small particles of dust will insinuate themselves into the mount. Such dust may be quite invisible to the unaided eye, but with high-power magnification may resemble rocks and boulders, possibly hiding completely some particular feature we wish to observe. Still, if the glass slips and cover-glasses are kept in their boxes and well polished before use with a soft cloth or piece of old silk, the stoppers or corks of bottles replaced without unnecessary delay after use, all glassware such as watch-glasses, petri dishes, beakers and, particularly, pipettes washed before being put away, the work-bench kept well dusted and everything either put away in a cupboard or covered with a sheet for the night, we shall be taking a few steps in the right direction.

System, too, will aid us in our efforts to avoid dust and dirt, but the nature of the system will depend largely on the individual and on the space and equipment at his command. I do not mean by this that in a large, well-equipped laboratory orderliness will come of its own accord or that on a corner of a bench in an outhouse there is bound to be confusion. There should be a place for everything and everything should be in its place; each item of equipment or of chemicals should be replaced at once in its rightful niche. This saves time and lessens the risk of breakages and of bottles being overturned. Another point of importance concerns the use of pipettes: have as many of these as you can afford and keep them in a rack, for they are the most convenient means of manipulating liquids, but if a pipette is used for, say, turpentine it should not be used for any other liquid without being cleaned. It is obvious that if this slovenly way is persisted in none of the chemicals will be absolutely pure in time.

The laboratory itself may be an elaborate affair or it may be but a humble soap box with a hinged lid and shelves added. The equipment, too, may range from a glittering array of instruments and glassware and polished mahogany cabinets to a few pipettes, watch-glasses and needles contained in an old cigar box. For a very modest outlay, however, in time a varied and useful assortment of instruments and chemical media can be acquired. The microscopist uses only a very small quantity of any particular medium at a time and so even a few penny-worths of almost any of the chemicals listed in this chapter will last a long time.

Equipment

The following list of implements and apparatus used in microscope slide making is by no means comprehensive, neither, by the same token, are they all essential; still, they facilitate matters. Some can be made at home with little difficulty.

Glass slips. These, of course, are essential. They are obtainable in various qualities but the size is standardized, viz., three inches long by one inch wide. It is surprising how very few chemists and opticians in the smaller towns keep a stock of glass slips. Fortunately they can be obtained by post quite cheaply from firms dealing in microscopes and accessories. Seven shillings will purchase half a gross of the cheaper kind, the better quality will cost twice as much and will be crystal white and somewhat thinner. Both qualities should have ground edges. Excavated slides will cost from sevenpence each according to the diameter of the excavation, this ranging from about seven and a half millimetres to eighteen millimetres. The prices for larger quantities are correspondingly less.

Cover-glasses. Cover-glasses also are essential no matter what type of mount is favoured. They are made of exceedingly thin glass and are cut either round or square in three sizes, $\frac{5}{8}$in., $\frac{3}{4}$in., and

⅜in.; other sizes can be cut to order. Also there are three degrees of thinness, viz., No. 1, very thin (approx. .15mm.) used for bacteriological work and where very high powers are used; No. 2, intermediate (approx. .21mm.) and No. 3 (approx. .3mm.), the last-named being a good, general utility cover-glass. The prices range from about eight shillings and threepence per ounce for the No. 3 size to fourteen shillings and sixpence per ounce for the No. 1 size. Prices for the squares are slightly less. The novice would be well advised to buy just half an ounce of the No. 3 size at first; there are quite a number in a half-ounce box, and leave the thinnest sizes until he is more accustomed to manipulating these very fragile little objects. Whilst on the subject of cover-glasses perhaps it would not be amiss to give some instruction on how to clean them. With practice even the thinnest can be cleaned by breathing on them and rubbing gently with a piece of silk between the ball of the thumb and the middle finger. This requires confidence and a light touch and a lot of practice. Another good way is to lay the glass on a flat surface, it must be absolutely flat otherwise the glass will break as soon as pressure is used, and rub each side with silk after it has been well breathed on. Another method is to cover two pieces of wood, each about two inches in diameter and half an inch thick, with chamois leather, bunching the leather on one side to make a kind of handle. Place a cover-glass on one pad and, by using a rotary movement, polish with the other pad. Experience will show that the first method is by far the quickest and best.

Pipettes. These, of various lengths and of different diameters, are listed by most dealers at from about fourpence to eightpence each. All else failing ordinary fountain-pen fillers serve quite well.

Watch-glasses. For treating objects in small quantities of liquid watch-glasses are invaluable. They have one great fault, however, they are so easily tipped over and for this reason the solid glass blocks are to be preferred. The price of the former is eightpence each and that of the latter two shillings and sixpence which includes a square glass cover.

Cells. For mounting objects in fluid or for other mediums when the object is rather thick, cells are required. They are made by attaching to a glass slide a ring of aluminium obtainable in several thicknesses ($\frac{1}{16}$in., $\frac{1}{24}$in., and $\frac{1}{32}$in.) and having the same exterior diameter as the standard cover-slips. These rings are punched out of sheet metal and as a result neither side is really flat; by

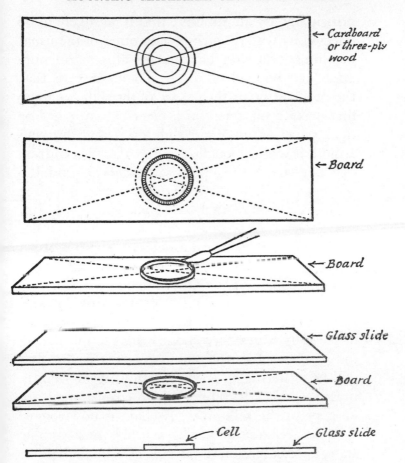

FIG. 13.—METHOD FOR ENSURING 'CELL' BEING IN CENTRE OF SLIDE

rubbing each side lightly on emery or glass-paper laid flat this can be rectified. The rings should be affixed to the centre of the slide, for neatness principally, by an adhesive that is not likely to be affected by water, spirit or any other of the usual mediums. Canada balsam, for all general purposes, answers admirably. To make sure that the ring will be in the centre of the slide we must first make a 'pattern' on a piece of cardboard or thick paper by laying a slide on it and drawing around it with a pencil (see Fig. 13). Then draw two lines from the opposite corners to find the centre and with a pair of compasses describe three circles with diameters of $\frac{5}{8}$in., $\frac{3}{4}$in., and $\frac{7}{8}$in. respectively. Now take a ring and place it in the circle having the same diameter and with a brush give the uppermost edge a thin coating of Canada balsam. Select a glass slip, making sure that it is not at all greasy, and lay it on the ring. If you look on top of it at the time it will be quite easy to see if its edges correspond with the outline on the pattern. Lift the slide over gently, the ring will be adhering to it, and with a needle lightly press the ring all round, this to ensure there are no gaps in the adhesive. A chain is no stronger than its weakest link, and a cell is in a similar state, a weak section in the ring of Canada balsam will be an invitation to the fluids to seep through, at that spot. Aluminium cell rings will cost one shilling and sixpence to two shillings a dozen.

A very thin cell can be made by applying a thin

ring of Canada balsam to the centre of a slide. The balsam will dry hard in time but when it is required for use another ring can be added. It is a good plan to prepare a number of different cells at a time, they can be stored with little difficulty and will save much annoyance when one is wanted in a hurry. Further details regarding cells will be found in the chapter 'Ringing, finishing and storing'.

Turntables. Unfortunately there is no satisfactory substitute for the turntable and, unfortunately again, slides cannot be efficiently or

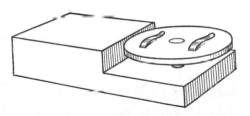

FIG. 14.—TURNTABLE

neatly finished without its aid. With practice, and a natural aptitude, I admit that a mount can be sealed and varnished by using a brush freehand but the result generally looks as though a child has smeared toffee over it. Basically, this instrument consists of a block of wood to which a metal disc is fitted horizontally. A pinion running from the centre of the disc fits into a sleeve supplied with ball-bearings. A flick of the finger should be sufficient to make the turntable spin for a minute at least. The cheapest turntable worthy of the name will cost fifty shillings.

Forceps. There are, literally, dozens of different types of forceps on the market, each with its own particular use. For general microscope work (manipulating cover-glasses and handling the larger objects) a straight pair with comparatively blunt points is best; but for picking up such things as the minute crustacea, the smaller moths and other insects, etc., a pair with fine points is very useful. Owing to the diversity of chemicals, some of them acid and rust producing, into which the forceps will at one time or other be placed, it is advisable to have them made from stainless steel. They will cost, if made of stainless steel, about six shillings and ninepence each.

Petri dishes. When fairly large quantities of fluid are to be used or for examining the contents of a tow-net or other pond life gatherings these glass dishes are most useful. They are quite flat on the bottom and about an inch high. A variety of sizes are available ranging from about an inch and a half in diameter to eight inches or more. Sold usually in pairs, one slightly larger than the other to act as a lid, at a cost of five shillings a pair or thereabouts according to the size.

Mounting needles. Needles mounted in holders are of inestimable service to the microscopist.

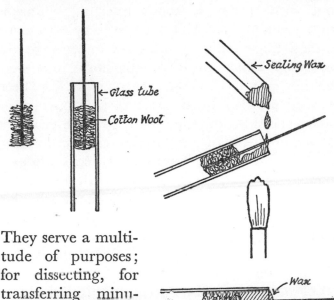

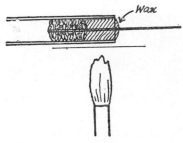

They serve a multitude of purposes; for dissecting, for transferring minutiae from one slide to another or to watch-glass or petri dish and for all manipulations that demand a light and sure touch. Although listed by

FIG. 15.—HOW TO MAKE A MOUNTING NEEDLE

most of the dealers they are quite easy to make at home, in fact there are certain types that are on no maker's list. Natural history books of a generation or so ago spoke glibly, but without detail, about inserting a needle in a penholder as being an easy way of making a mounting needle. I have yet to see a needle mounted either easily or efficiently in a penholder even when the sharp end has been pushed into the wood; and, of course, it is the sharp end that does the work. A far better way is to mount them in glass tubing obtainable from almost any chemist for about three shillings a pound. So cheaply can they be made and so useful is a variety of sizes that a set from a bodkin downwards should be aimed at. The glass tubing can be bought in several diameters, for the larger needles the $\frac{3}{8}$-in. diameter serves admirably.

Wrap the eye end of the needle with cotton wool so that when the wad of wool is pushed into the end of the glass tube the needle projects from its middle, and parallel with the sides of the tube (see Fig. 15). Stand the tube between two old books and then run sealing wax around the base of the needle. If the cotton wool does not come right up to the rim so much the better, the wax will run in and so make a more solid setting for the needle. Six inches is a convenient length for the tube. A piece of sealing wax run into the opposite end will prevent fluff, etc., from gathering in the tube and also give a 'finish' to the job.

For dissecting minute crustacea, etc., very fine needles are required, needles much finer than any you will find in a lady's workbox. For this purpose pins, as used by the entomologist for mounting mites, micro-pepidoptera and the like, are ideal. From the continent come rustless steel pins in the finer sizes but for general use the English pins suffice. A sample card of each of the ten sizes used by the entomologist will provide the material for the finer needles. If the points are rubbed lightly on an India stone a knife-like edge can be produced, sufficiently sharp for dismembering the small fry. Tubes of a narrower gauge are advisable for these fine pins.

Water-bath. A valuable adjunct to the laboratory equipment is the water-bath and its cost is negligible. Its principal use is for warming fluids or melting wax, jelly, glue and so forth. Any utensil that can withstand heat will suffice, an old, burnt saucepan served as my water-bath for many years; the outer part of a glue pot, virtually a water-bath in itself, is useful also. It may be used in two ways; three-quarters filled with water and placed over a flame and the jar containing the wax or whatever it is that is to be heated placed therein whilst still over the flame is the principal method; but another way, of particular value where there is no facility for a bunsen burner, is nearly to fill it with hot water and then insert the other receptacle. A fair number of substances can be melted by the latter means but some, glue for example, and shellac, require the surrounding water to be boiling for some little time.

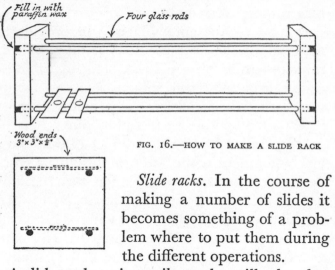

FIG. 16.—HOW TO MAKE A SLIDE RACK

Slide racks. In the course of making a number of slides it becomes something of a problem where to put them during the different operations.

A slide rack, quite easily made, will solve that problem (see Fig. 16). Take two pieces of wood three inches square and half an inch thick and in each drill four holes, all of them being three-quarters of an inch in from the sides adjacent.

Now take four glass rods (glass is better than iron or brass for this purpose as it is not affected by ordinary chemicals) of the same diameter as the holes, say three-eighths of an inch, and a foot in length. Insert these in the holes but do not push them right through, allow a space of about an eighth of an inch, then fill this space in with paraffin wax; this will give rigidity to the structure. The stand thus made will hold eleven slides on each of the two racks.

Slide boxes. Slides should be stored flat, never edgeways; for this reason most slide boxes consist of a number of trays with separate compartments for each slide. The price varies according to the capacity of the box and the material. Those with cardboard trays will cost fourteen shillings or so for a holding capacity of a hundred and forty-four. Unless one is particularly adept with hammer and saw there is little point in constructing them at home.

Specimen and storing jars and bottles. In principle any old jar or bottle, provided it is properly corked or stoppered, will serve to hold chemicals or to store specimens. The psychological effect, however, of an array of bottles of all shapes and sizes is a depressing one and, absurd though it may sound, far better work can be done when these containers 'look the part' than when they appear to have been rescued from a dustbin. If improvised bottles must be used then try to keep to one particular kind. By this I do not mean that one should sit up all night taking So and So's cough mixture in order to amass sufficient of their bottles. Use those that come to hand but discard them as soon as a more business-like bottle comes along. Specimens certainly should be stored in bottles or jars of a standard shape, they are easier to store and take up less room. Also avoid bottles with metal caps, they will rust away in time, allow the liquid to evaporate and so the specimens will dry up. Corks are far better and for the plutocrat there are those with ground glass stoppers. The diverse types of bottle are so great that it would be invidious to single out any individual type here. As a rule most types are quite inexpensive as a glance at a dealer's list will show.

The aforementioned items of equipment are but a few of those that are used by the microscopist at one time or another. Many can be dispensed with entirely, some can be made in the home, some are used or not used according to the fancy of the individual; this much I will say, however, a dealer's catalogue can be absorbingly interesting and instructive.

LABORATORY CHEMICALS

The chemicals mentioned in the following list are those most commonly used in mounting objects for the microscope. They are not all essential yet each has its own particular use, one medium may demand a technique that comes easier to one person than to another and some are cheaper than others.

The prices given, generally, are for the smaller quantities but in all cases the larger quantities are considerably less in proportion. Owing to the uncertain state of the markets through wars and so forth prices tend to fluctuate from time to time.

Alcohol. The microscopist has two great uses for alcohol, first as a preservative for nearly all organisms except the very delicate ones such as desmids and jelly-fishes, second as a dehydrating agent. It is with the latter quality that we are mostly concerned in the matter of mounting slides. Canada balsam cannot be used unless the object is entirely dehydrated, that is, the water driven off either by drying or by replacing it with a non-aqueous fluid. Alcohol accomplishes this very efficiently. Unfortunately the purchase of this commodity entails so much trouble in the matter of filling-in forms and so forth that if a substitute can be used so much the better. Moreover the price of absolute alcohol, owing to the heavy duty, is so exorbitant that the ordinary person cannot afford to buy it. Commercial alcohol, containing 90% spirit, is cheaper and is used, when diluted to 50% spirit, as a preservative; but it will not completely dehydrate. Cellosolve (q.v.) is a reliable substitute for pure alcohol.*

Ammonia. This alkali has several uses in microscope technique. It will dissolve certain animal and other tissues. When cleaning diatoms, for instance, if a few drops of ammonia are added to one of the later washings much of the flocculent matter will be eradicated.

Asphaltum. This is one of the pitches obtained from coal and for our use it must be the pure, genuine asphaltum. It is used for 'finishing' slides; a thin layer run round the edge of the cover-slip gives a black finish which also assists in keeping the cell airtight. For use it must be

---

*Industrial Methylated Spirit, water white and not tinted in any way, is 99.24%, that is to say, very nearly 'absolute'. Cedar or other clearing oil will dispose of the tiny fraction of water. This spirit costs about one shilling and fourpence a pint.

To obtain it, first write and apply to the local officer of Customs and Excise for permission to purchase 'Industrial Methylated Spirit' and state the purpose for which it is required, e.g., microscopical work and preserving specimens. The Customs will send a form which has to be filled up and returned to them. When they have received this they will issue a requisition book with perhaps three or four order forms in it; one of these is to be filled up on each occasion when it is desired to purchase the spirit, and the duplicate retained.

dissolved in linseed oil, turpentine or naphtha. A good preparation may be purchased quite cheaply containing india-rubber; such a preparation will dry quickly and will not crack or flake off easily.

Benzole, otherwise *Benzene*. This is also a product of coal; its great use is as a solvent of fats and oils. Material from which these are to be freed can be treated with benzole. The price is ninepence-halfpenny an ounce (liquid).

Bleaching fluids. When an object is too opaque to be mounted as a transparency it can, sometimes, be rendered transparent by treating it with a bleaching medium. One of the most simple to prepare consists of mixing a quarter of an ounce of chloride of lime in a pint of cold water. Shake the mixture well and allow to settle. After an hour or so the clear fluid may be poured off into a bottle and can be used as required. Another good bleaching fluid is peroxide of hydrogen obtainable from ironmonger or chemist for tenpence a four-ounce bottle. Chloride of lime can be bought at the same places in quarter-pound jars at a shilling.

Camphor water. For liquid mounts of very delicate nature the following mixture is valuable: a quarter of an ounce of tincture of camphor dissolved in a quart of distilled water and well

Plate XII

ROTIFERS AND INFUSORIA

1. *Bursaria vorticella.*   Freshwater infusoria.
2. *Chaetonotus larus.*   ,,   ,,
3. *Stentor Mulleri.*   ,,   ,,
4. *Euglina viridis.*   ,,   ,,
5. *Rotifer vulgaris.*   Freshwater rotifer.
6. *Chaetospira Mulleri.* ,,   ,,
7. *Vorticella microstoma.* ,,   ,,
8. *Synchaeta pectinata.*   ,,   ,,
9. *Brachionus Bakeri.*   ,,   ,,
10. *Vaginicola crystallina*   ,,   ,,
11. *Coleps hirtus.*   ,,   ,,
12. *Hydatina senta.*   ,,   ,,
13. *Monocera vattus.*   ,,   ,,
14. *Difflugia pyriformis.*   ,,   ,,
15. *Stephanoceros Eichornii.* ,,   ,,

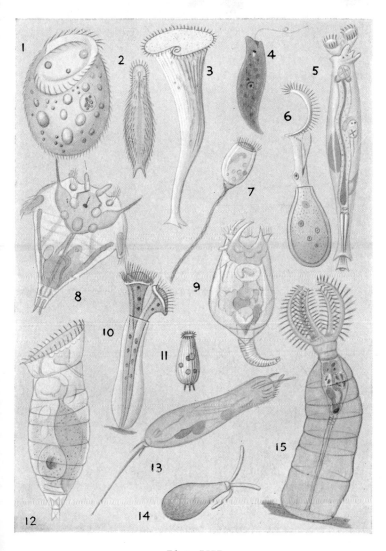

Plate XII

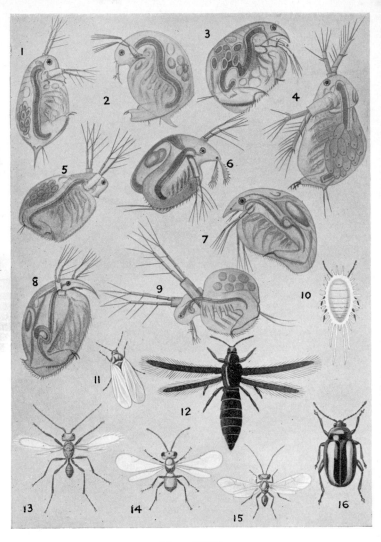

Plate XIII

PLATE XIII

FRESHWATER *CLADOCERA* (CRUSTACEANS) AND MINUTE INSECTS

1. *Daphnia pulex.* 3mm. The common 'Water Flea'. Cladocera.
2. *Bosmina obtusirostris.* 1mm. Cladocera.
3. *Eurycercus lamellatus.* 4mm. Cladocera.
4. *Sida crystallina.* 3mm. Cladocera.
5. *Simocephalus vetulus.* 3mm. Cladocera.
6. *Macrothrix laticornis.* 0.65mm. Cladocera.
7. *Acroperus harpae.* 1mm. Cladocera.
8. *Peracantha truncata.* 0.65mm. Cladocera.
9. *Moina branchiata.* 1.6mm. Cladocera. A very rare species.
10. Mealy Bug. 3/32″.
11. *Aleurodes vaporariorum.* Greenhouse White Fly. 1/25″.
12. *Frankliniella robusta.* Pea Thrip. 1/15″.
13. *Polynema natans.* Parasitic Chalcid.
14. *Telenomus bombycic.* Parasitic Proctotrypid.
15. *Cynips.* Gall-fly.
16. *Phyllotreta undulata.* Flea Beetle. 1/16″.

shaken up. Allow to settle and pour off the clear fluid into a bottle; this will be used for actually mounting the specimens. The cloudy liquid does very well for preserving them until they are ready to be mounted.

Canada Balsam. This is one of the finest mounting mediums known; it sets hard and so, save for effect, does not require ringing, with few exceptions does not injure delicate structures, and is clean to handle. One drawback, however, is that it takes a long time to dry and another that the object must be dehydrated first. Apart from that, this resin, for such it is, has been the standby of the microscopist for years and years. Canada balsam can be bought in a dry state and for use must be dissolved either in chloroform or xylol; sometimes alcohol, benzole or turpentine is used, but xylol seems to be the most popular solvent nowadays; bottles containing the balsam dissolved in any of the above can be obtained for about five shillings for a fluid ounce, that is, excepting in alcohol which is sixpence extra.

Cedarwood Oil. There are two types of cedarwood oil, a thin kind used for 'clearing' (see Chapter on 'Mounting') and a thick kind for use with oil immersion lenses. Either may be bought for two shillings a bottle.

Cellosolve, otherwise *Ethylene glycol mono-ethyl*

ether. As previously indicated cellosolve can be used in the place of alcohol as a dehydrating medium. It is comparatively cheap (sixpence a fluid ounce) and your chemist can get it through his wholesale manufacturing chemist, but it may take time before the order eventually gets through. Objects may be placed directly in it, then in oil of cloves or cedarwood oil and mounted straight away in balsam, moreover, stains can be added immediately the object is placed in it, a great saving of time. Owing to its extremely volatile nature as small a quantity as possible should be used at a time; any that is left in the watch-glass will evaporate before the next preparation is ready.

Cements (for sealing cells). The art of cell making is to provide an efficient sealing medium. There will be no leakage through either the cover-glass or the slide itself (unless they are cracked), the weak part being the edge of the cover-glass. The object, then, is to run a ring of some fluid-resisting material around that vulnerable part. To this end many kinds of cement have been evolved, very few of which, however, conform to the following specifications:—elasticity, toughness, durability, ease of use, cheapness and, of course, sealing or sticking power. Many are too hard and chip away after a while through being insufficiently elastic; some fall to pieces in time and some dissolve. Most dealers in microscope preparations sell their own particular proprietary cements and these, for the most part, are extremely good. To be on the safe side, however, it is well to use a proprietary cement first, then a layer of gold size or specially-prepared shellac and finish off with asphaltum. The principal reason why I advocate these made up cements is because to make similar preparations in the home would involve most of the household utensils, to the infinite disgust of the lady of the house, the cost would be no less and the result might be a hopeless mess.

Clove Oil. This oil is used, as cedarwood oil is used, for clearing preparations prior to their being mounted in balsam.

Distilled water. This costs about one shilling a quart and can be purchased from any chemist. Its chief use is in fluid mounting and as a medium in which to keep diatoms, desmids and other delicate organisms. Confervoid growths are likely to form in time unless deterrents are added. A lump of camphor in the bottle will dissolve very slowly, sufficient to make the water slightly camphorated; a drop of carbolic, too, will prevent growths.

Farrant's Medium. The great advantage of this

medium over glycerine jelly is that it can be used cold yet will assume a viscid state after being exposed to the air for a time. It is made from gum arabic and glycerine and there is no secret about its preparation:—four parts by weight of picked gum arabic in four parts of distilled water (camphorated), then add two parts of pure glycerine. No heat must be used in the preparation at all. Stir the mixture gently with a clean stick or glass rod at intervals until the gum is dissolved, then strain it through fine cambric previously wetted with cold water. This medium should be kept in a glass-stoppered bottle and, save for it being used cold, used in the same way as glycerine jelly.

Formalin (technically, the 40% solution of formaldehyde). Here indeed is a valuable asset to the laboratory. Low in price and easy to use as a preservative, formalin also has the advantage over alcohol of not removing colours so quickly. On pond or sea expeditions it is most useful, as a small phial will be sufficient to preserve the creatures in a number of collecting jars. At one time a 5% solution was used as a preservative, but it has been found that a 2% solution is sufficient. In order to arrive at the correct amount of water to add to the 40% solution to make it a 2% solution we can use the following formula which, incidentally, is of value in diluting alcohol and other concentrations.

The formula is $\frac{x}{y}-1$; X equalling the original percentage and Y the desired percentage. Therefore to dilute a solution from 40% to 2% add to each volume of the original solutio n $\frac{40}{2}-1$, that is to say 19 volumes of the diluting fluid.

Formalin should be kept in a corked bottle; the same thing applies to specimen bottles preserved in formalin, for even a weak solution will corrode a metal cap in no time. By the same token all implements of iron or steel should be well cleaned after being used with formalin.

Glycerine, Pure. In many instances glycerine is the perfect preservative but care should be taken that delicate objects are not placed direct from water into pure glycerine. It has a great affinity for water and so anxious is it to mix that it is no respecter of delicate tissues, they are brushed casually aside. Therefore they must be introduced by gradual stages, 20%, 40%, 65%, 80%, 90% and finally pure glycerine—a fiddling business altogether. It is a fine medium for fluid mounts of small insects.

Glycerine Jelly. This is one of the handiest and quickest of all mounting mediums. Whether, however, it is to be a good mountant or an exceedingly bad one depends upon how it is made, the proportion of glycerine to gelatine must be exact, for this reason alone it is advisable to obtain a bottle (one shilling and sixpence) all ready made up from a microscope firm. Colours, especially of mosses, are retained for many years in glycerine jelly mounts.

Gold Size. You may obtain this from the shop that supplies the painter and decorator with his materials. Old gold size is considered to have greater tenacity than fresh stock, but do not ask for 'old gold size' at the shop or the man will think you are suggesting that his stock is ancient. One must buy it and then let it become old of its own accord. It is very useful for making an additional coat over the ring of cement for liquid and semi-liquid mounts. The cost is trifling.

Gums. The principal use of the various gums to the microscopist is that of mounting objects dry. Wings and appendages of insects, diatoms, foraminifera, radiolaria, mosses, etc., can be mounted dry and gums are employed to stick them to the glass slip. *Gum Arabic* dissolved in cold water and the solution poured through a damp cloth to filter it is quite a good gum; a few drops of glycerine, say six, added to the solution is an advantage. To prevent fermentation a few drops of oil of cloves or cedarwood oil should be added. *Gum Dammar* dissolved in xylol is excellent for mounting diatoms dry, or indeed to take the place of balsam for the other type of mounting. *Gum Tragacanth*, obtained from various species of vetch, is occasionally used to affix objects to the slide. Gum Dammar, already dissolved in xylol, can be purchased for two shillings a bottle, Gum Arabic in lump form for one shilling an ounce and Gum Tragacanth mucilage for two shillings for a fairly large bottle.

Japan, black. This is a mixture of turpentine, linseed oil, gum and asphalt; it is useful for giving a final coat when ringing, and besides giving a professional 'finish' to the slide will assist in keeping the mount waterproof. Most ironmongers stock black Japan at about three shillings and sixpence per half-pint. Cellulose varnishes, obtainable in various colours, are an admirable substitute.

Paraffin, Liquid. As a substitute for glycerine for the preliminary or rough examination of objects this viscid fluid, also known as Medicinal Paraffin, is most useful.

Paraffin Wax. No microscopist should be without, at least, a small quantity of this most versatile wax. Its uses are legion and those connected directly with mounting are described in the chapter on that subject. One use is connected with examining fluid matter on a slide; in order to limit the fluid to the centre of the slide a line drawn round it with a piece of this wax will stop any spreading. Another use is for sealing jars containing specimens that are not likely to be wanted for some time. For this purpose some lumps should be placed in a small jam-jar and the jar placed in a warm water-bath, then, when the wax is sufficiently melted (120 degrees Fahrenheit is the usual melting point) it can be painted round the cork with a brush. Specimens from which sections are to be cut can be embedded in paraffin wax, thus greatly assisting the razor by giving body to the specimen. The thin sections when placed on the slide can, if necessary, have the wax dissolved away with benzol or xylol. Other uses will occur to the manipulator in the course of his labours. The price varies slightly according to the melting point, roughly the quality with a melting point of 110 degrees Fahrenheit will cost two shillings and sixpence a pound and that with a melting point of 140 degrees will cost a little more.

Turpentine. This is used as an intermediary in mounting in Canada balsam; that is to say, if a dry object, hair, fibre, foraminifera, small insect, etc., is allowed to soak in turpentine for some hours the risk of air-bubbles forming will be considerably lessened. Balsam mixes readily with it and after a few moments will replace the turpentine in the porous parts, otherwise, if it was not used the air would be imprisoned and so the slide would be ruined. There are other intermediaries that serve quite as well such as benzol, xylol, acetone, cellosolve, etc.; they are known also as 'solvents'. Turpentine is distilled from the resin of various species of conifer and is marketed in several degrees of purity; unless the very best grade is used the preparations will suffer. The grade as sold by the chemist is a pure one, nevertheless, it is advisable to say that it is required for microscope work. Incidentally, it is a good plan to make friends with your chemist, he can, and will, without exception almost, help you all he can.

Water-glass. A tin of this amazing substance will be sufficient to make many hundreds of slides. Ordinarily it is used, when diluted, for preserving eggs. Virtually it *is* liquid glass, for one of the bases in its manufacture is white sand or powdered quartz, substances used in glass making. Only in recent years has its value as a mountant been suspected and there is little doubt that in time it will be as popular as glycerine jelly. It has several drawbacks, these are referred to in the chapter on mounting.

Xylol. This is a coal-tar by-product and is

alternatively known as xylene. As a solvent for Canada balsam it is admirable, its other uses are described as they arise in the chapters on mounting. Sufficient to fill an ordinary medicine bottle will cost about two shillings, but here, as with other chemicals not ordinarily stocked by the retail chemist, the cost may be a trifle more as it will have to be ordered specially.

I. M. Puri's Medium for mounting tiny insects such as gnats, aphides, etc:

Mix at 80 degrees Centigrade the following: Water, 10 c.c.; Acetic Acid, glacial, 3 c.c.; Gum acacia, 8 gm.; Chloral hydrate, 70 gm.; Glycerine 5 c.c.

The result is a thin, viscous fluid which hardens after being exposed to the air for a day or so. The insect is placed on a glass slip, a drop of the medium placed over it and a cover slip gently lowered over the mount. Conversely, the insect can be placed into the drop.

CHAPTER X

(a) Dry Mounting

WE have now thoroughly cleared the ground and at last we are in a position to set about the actual mounting. Glass slips, with cells already affixed and some with just a ring of cement, have already been prepared and before us is the task of mounting some diatoms and foraminifera.

The foraminifera are slightly easier to mount so they will be treated first. A thin cell will be required or one that has had a ring of cement, several coats thick, described on its centre. The cell should be slightly thicker than the largest of the forams. It is essential that the object is thoroughly dry otherwise condensed water will form on the cover-slip, this will hinder the view considerably and also cause confervoid growth to form.

To proceed with the mounting, however; foraminifera, being on the small side, require but a very thin film of gum to stick them to the slide.

If the film is too thick they will be covered by it and the details of their delicate structure partially obliterated. Place a small drop of gum within the cell, and with a thin needle spread it over as large an area as possible, occasionally breathing on the film to prevent it drying in the process. When a sufficiently thin film has been obtained allow it to dry.

Now, foraminifera can be mounted as a strewn slide, that is to say, sprinkled haphazard over the gum and evened up with a fine needle, or individual specimens placed in some semblance of a pattern. For the former, assuming that we have a quantity of them in a tube or bottle, all we need do is to shake them over the adhesive as evenly as possible and then breathe heavily upon them. The moisture from the breath is sufficient to make the gum 'tacky' enough to hold the specimens. This type of slide is all right when a representative part of a gathering is required, but for type slides or slides that are to become part of a faunistic collection it is better for them to be mounted separately. The ideal slide consists of several specimens of the same species so mounted that each presents a different aspect to the lens; top, side and bottom, so to speak, for many of them look very different when seen from different angles. Conversely, a number of specimens can be mounted separately, in rows or in circles. The advantage gained here is that only forams are mounted, detritus, sometimes an unwelcome feature of strewn slides, is avoided.

A few forams should be shaken out on to a piece of black paper (such as photographic printing paper is packed in suits admirably); then, with a well-pointed and slightly-moistened brush, lightly touch one of the whitish specks and transfer it to the gum film. If the speck seems reluctant to leave the brush, then breathe slightly on the gum when it will be retained. To moisten and point the brush draw it across your lips using a slight twisting motion.

At first the specks will look very tiny indeed, but as I have remarked earlier in this book, the eye gets accustomed to its task, and after a while, with the larger species in particular, the various types can be recognized without the aid of a hand magnifier even. Nevertheless, a magnifying glass greatly facilitates matters. A stiff bristle, the end of which having been chewed a bit, mounted in a holder can be used instead of a brush.

When the slide has received its complement of specimens, and after it has been breathed upon, it should be placed in a warm place to dry. In the warm days of summer there is little difficulty on that score, the atmosphere sufficing to dry the mount. In winter the slide must be warmed by other means. A strip of metal heated over a flame, but not so that it is red-hot, serves very well; the slide can be laid on it for a minute or so and by then the moisture will be driven off. At this stage of the proceedings care must be taken that dust does not settle on the gum; if, for instance, the slide is to be left in a warm room to dry it should be placed in a box of some sort. The same thing applies if it is to be left for some time before having the cover-glass affixed.

The slide is now assumed to be as dry as it is possible for a slide to be, and the next operation is that of affixing the cover-glass. Using the turn-table run a thin layer of cement round the rim of the cell and lay the slide aside whilst the cover-glass is being cleaned. After cleaning the cover-glass lay it on a box with its rim just overhanging the edge, it can be picked up more easily by the forceps this way. Now, with the forceps, lightly grip the overhanging rim of the cover-glass; next place the side of the rim opposite to the one that the forceps are gripping on one side of the cell and gently lower the cover-glass on to the cell. Then, with a needle point 'gently but firmly' press all round the rim so that the layer of cement makes contact at all points. If the outside diameter of the cell is the same as the diameter of the cover-glass

Plate XIV

FORAMINIFERA

1. *Rotalia globulosa.*
2. *R. Beccari.*
3. *Textularia variabilis.*
4. *Miliolina seminulum.*
5. *Cristellaria rotulata.* Sussex chalk.
6. *Globigerina bulloides.*
7. *Dentalina gracilis.*
8. *Lagena sulcata.*
9. *Bulimina Buchiana.*
10. *Nodosaria radicula.*
11. *Textularia striata.* Gravesend chalk.
12. *T. barretti.*
13. *Polystomella umbilicatula.*
14. *Nodosaria radicula.*
15. *Rotalina Voltziana.*
16. *Cassidulina laevigata.*
17. *Pyrgo murrhina.*
18. *Valvulina palaeotrochus.*
19. *Rotalina oblonga.*
20. *Peneroplis pertusus.*

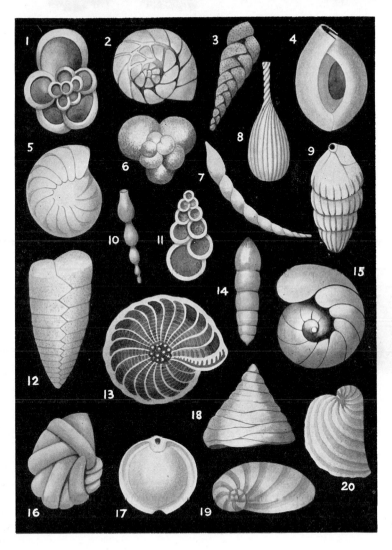

Plate XIV

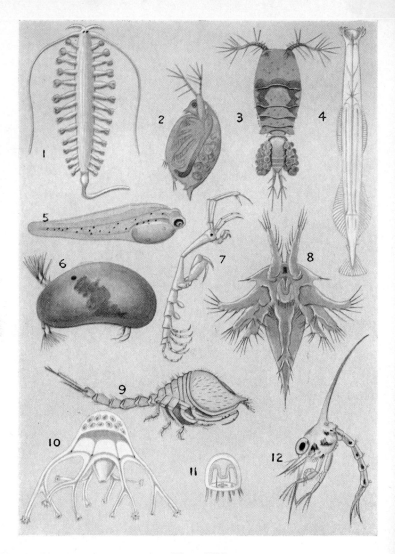

Plate XV

PLATE XV

MARINE PLANKTON AND MINUTE FRESHWATER CRUSTACEA

1. *Tomopteris onisiiformis.* Marine planktonic worm.
2. *Daphnia pulex.* A freshwater Cladoceran.
3. *Oncaea mediterranea.* A female planktonic copepod. Marine.
4. *Sagitta hexaptera.* One of the planktonic Arrow Worms.
5. Larval fish (Whiting).
6. *Cypris fusca*, an Ostracod.
7. *Caprella* sp. The crustacean Ghost Shrimp.
8. Larval stage of Acorn Barnacle, *Balanus balanoides.*
9. *Diastylis Goodsiri*, a planktonic Cumacean crustacean.
10. *Clavatella prolifera.* One of the medusa jelly-fishes.
11. *Microhydra ryderi.* One of the medusa jelly-fishes.
12. Zooea of *Carcinus maenas*, the Common Shore Crab.

the finished work should have a neat appearance, the cell entirely covered and no part of the cover-glass overhanging. The slide can be put away now, in a box, until it is ringed and finished.

Some objects, especially the larger forams, are too opaque when mounted dry to be viewed with transmitted light. With top light, however, they can be seen to greater advantage. When top light alone is to be employed all light from beneath must be blocked out, otherwise the effect is only half-hearted. To do this cut a disc of black paper, its diameter the same as that of the cell, and stick it on the underside of the slide directly beneath the cell. Gum Arabic, to which a few drops of glycerine have been added or failing that a few grains of sugar, is a satisfactory adhesive for this purpose; without the glycerine or sugar, though, the paper would fall off in time.

The directions for mounting forams can be followed when any other dry material is to be mounted; the wings of the many species of fly found in the garden or hedgerow, small pieces of butterfly wings, petals of flowers, mosses, appendages of insects and, in many cases, the whole insect, and many other objects can be made into delightful preparations. A complete dissection of a shrimp, a small one that was hardly worth eating at teatime can be used, is at once interesting and instructive, especially if a text book such as Huxley's *Crayfish* is consulted as the work progresses. The crayfish is built along very similar lines to the shrimp and the prawn, consequently, as each appendage is removed it can be compared with the illustrations in the book and correctly named. Fine-pointed scissors or forceps can be used for the actual dissection. If the specimen is placed in a $2\frac{1}{2}\%$ solution of caustic potash (a small bottle of this will cost about one shilling from the chemist) for an hour the various parts will separate more easily. Hold the body of the shrimp with blunt forceps held in the left hand then, with needle-point forceps manipulated with the right hand, gently tug each appendage until it is torn away from the integument connecting it with the main part of the body. Start with the head region, detaching the antennae first, then the broad, leaf-like 'scale', then each successive pair of legs and finally the tail (incidentally this makes quite an attractive subject for the microscope). We have yet to remove the appendages surrounding the mouth, that is, the lips and the pair of legs that the shrimp utilizes as teeth. The mouth appendages are rather small, but not microscopically so.

Before mounting the appendages, we shall require a separate slide for each pair, the caustic potash must be washed out of the tissues, likewise the small amount of flesh contained in the legs. Place each pair in turn in a watch-glass containing water, distilled if at all possible, and gently brush them with a soft brush. The potash will have dissolved what little flesh there is and the brush should squeeze it out. Remove the first lot of water with a pipette, not disturbing the preparation, and add another wash of water. Repeat the operation yet once again and by then all the potash should be washed out. With the forceps remove the legs, just touching them with filter or blotting paper to dispose of the excess water, and place them on the slide, having prepared it previously with a thin smear of gum. The antennae can, with patience, be curled round and mounted like a flat spiral; the legs can be bent naturally so that the cell will accommodate them. If they are too large for the largest circular cover-glass then we must use a rectangular one. Rectangular cover-glasses in all sizes up to two and a half inches long by seven-eighths wide can be bought for seven shillings for half an ounce. When square or rectangular covers are used the cell must be built up by putting layer upon layer of cement until the required thickness is attained. The final result, no matter how hard you try, is never as neat as a circular cell.

The appendages may refuse to lie down in the cell, being too springy for the gum to hold. To combat this a slight pressure must be put on the cover-glass to keep the preparation in place until it is definitely stuck down. For this purpose spring clips (Fig. 20) can be obtained. These clip on to one end of the slide, the other end of the clip resting on the centre of the cover-glass; the pressure can be regulated by bending the clip. In the absence of a clip I have found that a small cork just resting on the cover-glass will provide sufficient pressure. When the slides are finished off properly each can be labelled and the particular appendages named. Uncooked shrimps make better preparations than do the cooked ones, the colour cells, as a rule, are ruined and these are, perhaps, the most attractive part of the preparation.

Other creatures can be treated in a similar fashion, the shrimp is given, in rough and ready fashion, it is true, to show how the job should be tackled and how the method of dry mounting can be applied other than for minute objects.

There are two ways of mounting diatoms dry; they may be mounted on the slide or on the inside of the cover-glass. For mounting on the slide proceed as follows. well agitate the bottle containing the diatoms and with a dip-rod or pipette draw off a small quantity, little more than a couple of drops, of the fluid in which they are preserved. Place this within the cell, gently shaking the slide so that the fluid spreads evenly. Now, with a hot-plate or heated metal strip, dry the slide. In the ordinary way the diatoms will stick to the glass without the aid of gum, if they do not stick then the merest suspicion of gum may be used. Diatoms, being so minute, will require the shallowest cell possible, just one layer, two at most, of cement will provide the necessary depth. A ring of cement is now run around the rim of the cell and the cover-glass affixed in the usual way. Many diatoms are so remarkably minute that only the highest powers can make anything of them and with these high-powers the lens has to be very close to the diatom. Therefore the thinnest of cover-glasses are used and, further to lessen the distance, they are mounted direct on to the cover-glass. The actual procedure differs but little from that used when mounting on the slide; the liquid containing the diatoms is placed on the cover-glass and evaporated quickly. Some authorities favour actually making the glass red-hot, the idea being that all dross is burned away, leaving brilliantly clear specimens, which definitely adhere to the glass. This method might be all right for robust specimens but I doubt whether the more delicate species would survive.

The aforementioned methods, of course, produce 'strewn' slides; to mount individual specimens, transferring them by means of bristle or brush, one has to be an artist. Yet I have seen many slides of diatoms in which hundreds, literally, of these infinitesimally minute motes, have been arranged in all manner of delightful patterns, the results of weeks of patient labour. It is only on the few that this gift is bestowed and I 'looks towards them and I likewise bows'; they are unheralded and unsung yet their labours are of incredible value, especially when they turn their attention to pathological microscopy and its allied subjects.

So much for dry mounting. There are two things that must be kept in mind all the time and I make no excuses for repeating them; they are, do not affix the cover-slip until the mount is absolutely dry, and, keep out dust!

(b) Wet Mounting

In wet mounting the object must first be well saturated in the same medium in which it is to be mounted or in a medium that has an affinity with the mounting medium. In all cases the medium is in a fluid state at first, later hardening completely as Canada balsam does and water glass when in a dry atmosphere, or partially hardening as glycerine jelly, Farrant's Medium, etc., do when kept in cool, dry conditions.

For the purpose of comparison between the various ways in which the different mediums must

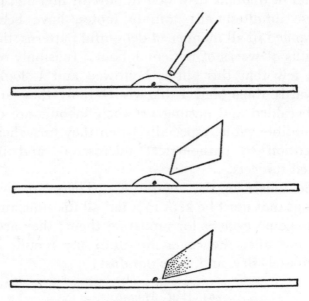

FIG. 17.—REMOVING MOISTURE FROM SPECIMEN

be used we will, in all cases, take it upon ourselves to mount cyclops, a very common inhabitant of almost any pond.

Glycerine Jelly. Our gathering of cyclops, having been killed previously by adding formalin to the water, is at hand. With a pipette a specimen or two is laid on the centre of a glass slide. With a piece of filter paper as much moisture as possible is removed and, by using the pattern described on page 180 the specimens are pushed gently into the centre of the slide, using a mounted needle for the purpose. Glycerine jelly, when cold is more or less solid, consequently it must be warmed by placing the bottle containing it in a water-bath until it is fluid. Do not get it too hot otherwise the object will be distorted, use it as cool as possible, while yet liquid. The cork of the bottle should be pierced so that a glass rod can be inserted (see Fig. 18), thus when the bottle is corked the rod is inside. When the jelly is fluid enough to permit it, just ease the cork out, otherwise, especially if the water-bath is being heated over a bunsen burner, the bottle might burst when it gets hot.

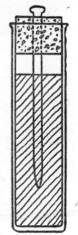

FIG. 18.— GLYCERINE BOTTLE, SHOWING DIP-ROD FIXED THROUGH HOLE IN THE CORK

The jelly is now sufficiently fluid and so the cork, and, of course, at the same time the glass rod is withdrawn and a drop of the fluid placed over the cyclops (see Fig. 19). The amount of jelly required will depend on the thickness of the object and the diameter of the cover-glass to be used. In time one can judge to a nicety how much will be required. In the meantime a cover-glass

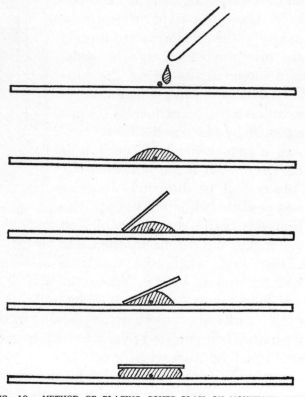

FIG. 19.—METHOD OF PLACING COVER-GLASS ON MOUNTANT WITH GLYCERINE JELLY

should have been cleaned and placed just over-lapping the edge of a box so that the forceps can pick it up conveniently. Holding it by the edge with the forceps just pass it through the flame of a bunsen burner, not too quickly and not too slowly, then breathe on the side that is to have contact with the jelly. Glycerine has a great affinity for moisture and the thin film of moisture deposited by the breath will help to avoid air bubbles; also, the flame will burn up any small bits of fluff and so forth that may have settled on the cover after it was cleaned. Now, holding the cover on the right-hand edge gently place the left-hand one slightly to the left of the blob of jelly, gauging it so that, when the cover is lowered, the cyclops will be in the centre. Do not lay the cover flat on the jelly; hold it at an angle of 45° and lower it until the jelly strikes the cover, then slowly reduce the angle until the cover lies flat on the slide.

Maybe the jelly does not occupy the whole of the underside of the cover and the space thus formed must be filled in; to do this do not put the jelly where the space is, unless of course it runs entirely round the edge, but just touch with the glass rod, loaded with warm jelly, at the junction of the jelly that has reached the edge and the space. The jelly will then run in without forming air bubbles. Maybe, the cyclops does not occupy the centre of the slide; in this case, so that we do not have to make the slide all over again we can tilt the slide, when the jelly has set somewhat, in the direction we want the object to move. Its weight, such as it is, will cause it to precipitate itself, slowly it is true, towards the centre.

Air bubbles, the bugbear of the microscopist, may form, no matter how carefully the rules are followed. They arise from various causes; through the object not being sufficiently saturated in the first place, through bubbles of air forming in the mounting medium, which they do if it is agitated by shaking or through the cover-glass being lowered ineptly. To remove them we must take a stoutish needle and make it red hot in a flame. The heat will soon go out of the needle, that is why a stout one is suggested, so the flame will have to be near at hand. Now, assuming that the jelly has set more or less, stroke the cover-glass with the point of the hot needle, working from the bubble to the nearest edge. The bubble, being light, will tend to rise, so incline the slide with the edge nearest the bubble uppermost. Gradually, maybe after heating the needle several times, the bugbear will move upwards towards the edge. When it reaches the edge a touch with the needle will make it burst. The heat from the needle causes the jelly to melt and so there is less resistance to the upward passage of the bubble.

The jelly soon sets if placed where it is cool. If

a number of slides are to be made place each, when the bubbles, if any, have been disposed of, in a box away from the dust. When the batch of slides has been made the next operation may be attended to and this consists of removing any excess jelly from the slide. It is almost impossible to gauge the exact amount of jelly required to run to the edge of the cover-glass, consequently there is usually a considerable excess and this, before the slide can be finished properly, must be removed. With a knife scrape this excess away making as clean a cut as possible round the edge of the cover-glass. The ringing cement will not adhere properly if there is the slightest trace of glycerine on the slide and the knife will not, in any case, remove all the jelly. Take a piece of soft cloth and moisten it in water and wipe firmly over the whole of the slide, working as near to the edge of the cover as possible without actually touching it. Several applications may be necessary before the glass is absolutely clean. The top of the cover-glass, too, may have a blob or smear of jelly on it; very gently scrape as much away as you can with a knife and then, even more gently, wipe over it with the damp cloth. Thoroughly dry all the parts that have been moistened and store the slide away until the time comes for it to be 'finished'.

Glycerine, as previously stated, has an abnormal affinity for water and will even attract moisture from the atmosphere which settles on the cover-glass in beadlets; moreover, the small amount of water with which our cyclops was saturated will work through the jelly and be precipitated in a similar manner. So keep the slides in as dry, and cool, a place as is convenient for a few days, drying off any beadlets that form with filter paper. When no further moisture forms the slides are ready for the final touches.

Farrant's Medium demands the same actual technique as that used with glycerine jelly, the main difference being that this medium must not be heated, it is used cold just as it is taken from the bottle. Exposure to the atmosphere will, in a few days, cause it to set, if not hard, at least sufficiently solid to permit excess material being wiped away and the slide cleaned as previously described. Otherwise its use is exactly the same as for the other jelly.

Water-glass has only been known within recent years as a mounting medium and, while the perfect mountant has yet to be found, I am convinced that for all ordinary purposes this remarkable material is ideal. The finished mount is glass-clear and the colour of the subject does not seem to be affected. Time, of course, is the deciding factor in that respect but my own preparations made somewhat over a year ago are as fresh looking as the day they were made; the colour cells of small crustaceans, which most mountants seem to destroy in time, are as bright as ever.

A tin purchased from the chemist will suffice for many hundreds of slides. Before opening it wipe carefully round the lid with a clean, damp cloth in order to remove any dust that may be lurking there. Now take a wide-mouthed jar, it need not be very large, say four inches high and an inch and a half in diameter, and threequarters fill it with water-glass, a spoon seems to be the best implement for the task. Then make up with water half of the remaining quarter. The water will gradually mix with the treacly fluid without stirring. Indeed, the act of transferring it to the jar will imprison hundreds of air bubbles and stirring will only increase the number. Stand the jar in a warm water-bath for several hours, this will help to drive off the bubbles and will assist in the mixing.

This medium can be used undiluted, especially if a largish object is to be mounted, but the risk of multitudes of air bubbles forming is very great.

For use, stand the jar in warm water (the chance of bubbles forming is thereby lessened) and proceed as with glycerine jelly. It will not set so quickly as that medium, however, and will remain 'running' for some time. Consequently, if the object is at all thick, further fluid must be added at the edges of the cover. Also, the object must be well soaked in water before it is mounted. The slide will require gently warming for some time before the water-glass will set sufficiently to be trimmed up. Room temperature, although it will do so in time, is hardly high enough to set it; on the other hand, if too high a temperature is applied, the surface will set in a tough, ruckled skin beneath which it is still quite fluid.

When the preparation is a very thin one less fluid will be used and so it will set quicker. For thick objects, however, whether water-glass, glycerine jelly, Farrant's or any other medium is used, a cell really is necessary.

The object is placed within a cell of the necessary depth and, by means of a pipette or dip-rod, the medium is introduced. Do not completely fill the cell with liquid, when the cover-glass is applied the meniscus formed by surface attraction may cause the liquid to overflow. The top of the meniscus should be just above the rim of the cell. Nevertheless, the cell must be filled otherwise a large bubble of air will form. Air bubbles nearly always occur when the medium is placed in the cell, this is due to the medium not running into the angle between the cell and the slide very well and to the fact that the transfer agitates it somewhat. Place only a little in at first and, with a needle, smooth it into the aforesaid angle, bursting the bubbles with the needle point as they form. Then add the rest and allow the slide to stand for a few minutes before putting the cover-glass on; if any further bubbles are to develop they can then be dealt with without

FIG. 20.—MOUNTING CLIP

having to remove it. The cover-glass should be manipulated and lowered as previously explained. When it is finally in place, if one's judgment has been good, there should be just a small oozing of the medium at its juncture with the cell. Press lightly all round with a needle and apply a weak spring-clip to the centre so that it is still touching the cell rim when the medium sets (see Fig. 20).

We come now to the gentle art of mounting with Canada balsam and here a slightly different technique is required. The object, before it is mounted, must be completely dehydrated; the slightest trace of water in the finished preparation will cause the balsam to turn cloudy to the ruination of everything.

Before bringing forth the cyclops to be mounted we must first 'set our stall out', bearing in mind that on the one hand we have our cyclops in water and, on the other hand, we have a medium that dislikes that element intensely. Alcohol is the agent we will employ, in this instance, as the connecting link; but we cannot place our water-logged cyclops directly into absolute spirit; like glycerine, alcohol has a great affinity for water, and may tear the cyclops asunder in its anxiety to extract it. The spirit we are using is the Industrial Methylated Spirit mentioned on page 190 and it must be broken down to each of the following strengths—30%, 50%, 70% and 90%. So five bottles of spirit will be set out in a row on the work-bench—one bottle is for the absolute spirit. Also on the bench we shall require the bottle of thin cedarwood oil (or oil of cloves) for this is the step between the absolute alcohol and the Canada balsam. If the specimen has been preserved in anything other than spirit we shall require some distilled water.

Place the cyclops in a watch-glass and remove with the pipette as much of the attendant liquid as possible. Now run in a pipetteful of distilled water; remove this with the aforesaid pipette and give the cyclops another wash in water. Draw off the water, taking care to leave the specimens behind in the watch-glass, and then place some of the 30% spirit therein. After about half a minute draw this off and replace it with 50% spirit and so on until the much harassed cyclops reposes in the absolute spirit. Its troubles are not over yet, however; draw off as much spirit as possible and then add the clearing oil. There is still a trace of water and so the watch-glass and its contents are placed in a warm spot for twenty-four hours or until there is no cloudiness in the oil. The warmth, of course, tends to evaporate the water. The warmth, however, must not be great, round about blood heat is the best, though slightly greater heat will do no damage. In the absence of the right appliance (an incubator) I can think of nothing better than the airing rack that is usually fixed above the kitchen range. If there is neither airing rack nor kitchen range then that's just too bad and one must look around for a satisfactory answer to the problem. A biscuit tin placed on a tray of sand on the side of the stove is sometimes satisfactory, or placed over a bunsen burner turned low. The tray of sand prevents the tin from becoming too hot and also assists in keeping an even temperature. This is an instance where the microscopist has to use his

227

own ingenuity; meaning, really, that I do not know of a satisfactory substitute for the rather expensive incubator.

However, having solved the problem to our satisfaction, we have, in the watch-glass, our cyclops completely dehydrated. They have now to be transferred to the centre of a slide and we must bear in mind that the specimens now are very brittle indeed. With the faithful pipette gather up the specimens and deposit them with the attendant oil on the slide. Filter or blotting paper will soon absorb the oil for us.

Close at hand is the cover-glass already cleaned and polished and so, with a glass rod, a drop of the balsam is placed on the object and the cover-glass applied in the usual way; in this instance the cover-glass is neither warmed nor breathed upon. The balsam will dry of its own accord in time but, unless the object is likely to be injured, warmth should be applied. Generally speaking, the quicker the balsam dries the harder it sets. As it dries it will shrink and this shrinkage must be made up as the drying progresses by placing a drop of balsam at the edge of the cover-glass, taking care that air bubbles do not form in the process. A warm oven will serve to dry the slide, but it should be placed in a box first to avoid dust. Before the balsam has actually set hard remove that which has overflowed on to the slide or the cover. To do this dip a piece of cloth in xylol and wipe it away; it may take some moments before the balsam is softened, but with perseverance a clean slide will result. If a large quantity has spread over the slide a pen-knife should be used first to scrape it away, also, with a knife a cleaner edge round the cover-glass can be made. The knife will not remove it all, however, so the xylol must be used for the rest.

Setting so hard as it does and not being affected by the atmosphere, whether wet or dry, a balsam mount does not require a cement ring. Nevertheless, to give uniformity to the collection, a ring of gold size followed by one of black Japan, asphaltum or a black cellulose varnish is advisable.

(c) Fluid Mounting

In fluid mounting the object is placed in a medium that always remains in a liquid state and does not harden or even become the slightest bit viscous. The fluid must contain a preservative of some sort which, whilst keeping bacteria, etc., at bay will not interfere with the mount itself. Distilled water to which has been added a fractional proportion of carbolic, camphor, thymol, formalin, phenol or toluol is the most usual medium. A very good mounting fluid consists of equal parts of water, glycerine and alcohol but this should not be used for the tiny jelly-fishes, zoophytes, hydroids or other coelenterates as the alcohol has a deleterious effect upon them.

The basic principle of fluid mounting is that the fluid is absolutely protected from outside influences, in other words, contained within a cell through which the fluid cannot escape or the atmosphere enter.

First of all there must be a cell ring the thickness of which will vary according to the thickness of the object to be mounted. This may be one or more thicknesses of cement placed on the centre of the slide, the diameter depending on the actual size of the object, commensurable with the standard cover-glass sizes; or an aluminium cell-ring cemented to the slide (Fig. 13). But whether the cell is merely made of cement or is cemented on, its success depends entirely upon the quality of that cement, and for this reason I advise the purchase of cements advised by the various dealers in microscope requisites. In many instances they have stood the test of time and are used by those same firms in the preparation of their own slides.

Excavated slides are admirable for mounting the smaller organisms in fluid. The excavation, in which the object has been placed previously, is filled with the mounting fluid and a cover-glass of suitable size, the edge of which has received a coating of cement, placed over it. With a needle press the cover down all round so that the cement adheres at all points. Wipe away all liquid that has extruded over the slide and put it away to be finished as soon as opportunity permits.

For other cells the procedure is very similar. A coating of cement is run round the rim, the object and the fluid introduced and the cover-glass pressed down so that the cement makes a good contact all round. Wipe off excess moisture and store away in a dry place.

Another, and most efficient, type of cell can be made with paraffin wax. (See Fig. 21). It also has the advantage of speediness; when a cell is required at once, and a cement one has not been made beforehand, paraffin wax can be used.

First of all take a lump of the wax, about the size of a walnut, and melt it over a flame on a sheet of glass. The wax will run out into a thin sheet. Plunge the whole into cold water when the wax will set hard; insert a knife under the edge of the sheet and lever it up. The sheet of wax can then be broken into pieces about a quarter of an inch square, those not required for immediate use can be stored in a cool, dry place.

Break the pieces up into still smaller pieces and

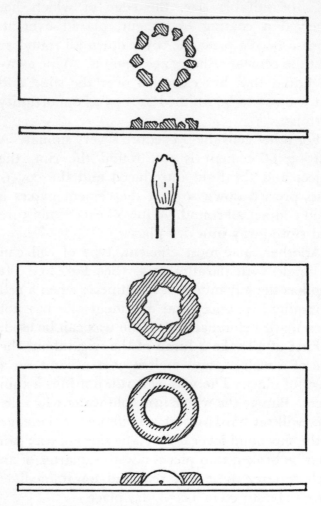

FIG. 21.— CELL MADE WITH PARAFFIN WAX

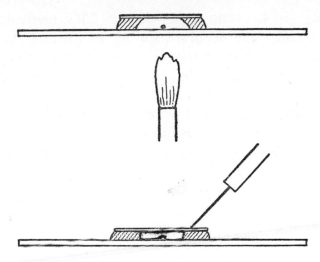

FIG. 21.—CELL MADE WITH PARAFFIN WAX

place them in a circle on a slide. It is difficult to say exactly how large this circle must be, but the operator must bear in mind that it must not be greater than the diameter of his cover-glasses. Now gently warm the slide; the pieces of wax will melt and run into one another leaving in the centre a somewhat battered-looking circle, which can be trimmed with a knife. Fill this with the liquid and, of course, the object. Then lay a cover-glass over the whole and apply some more heat, at the same time pressing lightly on the cover. It is but a matter of a few seconds only before the wax has melted and, at the same time, stuck to the cover-glass. This method, when once the accurate timing in melting the wax has been mastered, is of inestimable value. The mount, naturally, will require finishing with the usual cement.

A liquid mount that never fails to amaze one's friends and which gives intense satisfaction, when successfully accomplished, to the microscopist is that of a larval, or very small adult, fish that has been rendered transparent all save the bones which are stained a deep crimson. In the first place it is necessary to procure a small fish; the tow-net used in the sea in May or June should capture larval fishes under three-quarters of an inch in length, failing that there should be at about that time or just before, baby fishes in the pond. Conversely, if a friend happens to keep tropical fishes, when one of the smaller members of his aquarium dies, then that will make a satisfactory subject.

There are several methods employed in achieving this mount, but perhaps the best is that known as the Schultz method. The fish is placed in tincture of iodine or a saturated solution of potassium iodide overnight, in the dark. Then, with 70% alcohol it is washed in a watch-glass until no yellow comes away. From the 70% alcohol it is taken down by degrees (50% then

30%) to distilled water. The next step, after removing as much of the water as possible with the pipette, is to add a 1% solution of caustic potash (KOH) to the watch-glass at the same time adding a few grains of alizarin stain to the depth of port wine colour. Leave the specimen in this overnight. On the following day wash the fish in several changes of caustic potash until no stain comes away. Then add a few drops of ammonia, this to prevent yellowing of the muscles. The fish may be one that has rather distinct colour cells; to remove these add also a few drops of hydrogen peroxide (H_2O_2). Wash the poor creature again in caustic potash and then, by degrees bring it into pure glycerine, the steps being 25%, 50% and 75% glycerine. Throughout these performances the fish has not left the watch-glass; indeed, so wearied has it become, that it is a hazardous business to transfer it to the pure glycerine (to which a grain of camphor has been added) that occupies the cell. A section lifter, or failing that, a very thin strip of metal such as tin or lead foil, should be used. The finished mount is well worthy of the trouble that has been taken. The art is in timing the various operations. There is little difficulty about the first three, the difficult part is regarding the soaking in caustic potash; this will vary according to the bulk of the fish, a week being sufficient for a very tiny one and six months not too long for a largish specimen.

Nevertheless, the microscopist who can produce a good mount of this nature has indeed earned his spurs.

(d) Staining and section cutting

There are a very great number of stains used in microscopy, especially by the laboratory technicians in hospitals. The idea is to show up particular types of tissue or particular parts of the cell so that they stand out clearly when magnified. Thus methylene-blue will stain nerves a deeper blue than it will other structures; alizarin stains calcareous matter a rich red, and so on. Each kind of stain has its own particular virtue and it is possible to stain a preparation so that one piece of structure is red, say, and then, after well washing the section or object, stain with green, or blue or yellow. This is called 'differential' staining and it can produce some gaily coloured results, although the pathologist is not so interested in that aspect of it.

Many methods of staining demand an exacting technique, very often long and involved. To deal at all adequately with the subject would be far beyond the scope of the present volume; but there are numerous books devoted expressly to the subject and I venture to believe that by the time the beginner has read thus far he, or she, should be able to understand the technical language used.

Nevertheless, I propose here, in order to give some idea of the process, to describe a typical staining and section cutting routine.

We will assume we are interested in the nerve structure in the liver of a herring. First of all, of course, we remove the liver from the herring and allow a gentle stream of water to run over it whilst it is in a trough or dish. This is to clean it thoroughly, and this takes several hours. The next step is to immerse it in Bouins fluid in order to 'fix' the living tissues and cells. This fluid may be purchased already made up but it may be made from the following formula—picric acid, saturated aqueous solution, 75 parts; Formol, 25 parts; acetic acid, 5 parts.

The liver stays in this for from 12/16 hours, but not longer than 18 hours. It is then washed in 50% alcohol until all signs of the picric acid have gone. Two hours after being in this bath it is placed in 70% alcohol for two hours and then for a further two hours in absolute alcohol. When removed it is placed in a bath of cedarwood oil and removed from this and placed in yet another, and finally in a third. This is to make sure there is not the slightest trace of water in it.

The piece of herring is now placed in a jar containing paraffin wax heated to 52 degrees Centigrade, then into a second, and then removed from that into a third. This is so that the paraffin wax has thoroughly impregnated it. It is then placed in a small jar of melted wax and the whole plunged into cold water to set. From the jar, after trimming to a workable size, it is transferred to the section cutter. This consists of a machine in which there is an 'open' razor and a piece to hold the wax embedded tissue. This piece, usually, has an up and down movement against the edge of the blade. By pushing a lever back and forth this movement is produced and at the same time the 'piece' is advanced a little at a time. Ideally, the sections leave the blade in the form of a ribbon, the edge of one section touching the edge of the next.

We are now about half-way there.

We have by us at this stage a row of glass slides and on the centre of each we have smeared a mixture consisting of white of egg 50 parts and glycerine 25 parts. This sticks the section to the slide and the section, it will be noticed, consists of quite a lot of paraffin wax and this must be removed. The slides, therefore, are placed in two successive baths of xylol to achieve that end.

NOTE.—From now onwards until the mount is finished the slides must be kept moist. This is not only important—it is essential.

Unless otherwise stated the different operations, such as working up or down in different strengths of alcohol, etc., consist of little more than immersing the slide in the particular strength for only a few seconds. The section is so thin that soaking is unnecessary.

From the xylol the specimen is taken down through 90%, 70%, 50% and 30% alcohol to distilled water and then stained with haematoxalin for half an hour. A small portion of the stain is added to distilled water until it is of a rich, reddish colour and the slide placed in it. Then the slide is dipped into two successive baths of tap water; the salts in this kind of water fix the stain. Then into distilled water again and from there by the stages already given to absolute alcohol. There should be two successive baths of the absolute alcohol. Then into two xylol baths until clear of all traces of water and mounted in Canada balsam and xylol.

A long, complicated process you may think. Yet operations of this nature, when the necessary equipment and the chemicals in their different strengths are already prepared, are simplicity itself.

Of course, the sections may be cut by hand with a razor. A few only of these sections will be sufficiently thin for the purpose, but unless a complete series is required they should suffice.

(e) Drawing under the Microscope

Very often we come across an object that we feel we should like to draw, possibly with a view to taking our drawing to an expert for identification or, as is frequently the case, we are studying some particular subject and want to make a collection of drawings for our own reference. In the ordinary way the microscope slide itself is sufficient for our purpose but this is not always the case. The object of our study might be such as will not make a good preparation—pollen is one such —or we may wish to illustrate a monograph or some other form of 'write up'.

For about fifteen guineas we may purchase an accessory designed to enable us to make such drawings. This is the camera lucida. It is fitted to the eye-piece end of the draw-tube and one part consists of a hinged mirror so that it can be inclined at different angles. A sheet of paper is placed on the table at the side of the microscope and immediately below the mirror. Sometimes the paper will have to be tilted as well as the mirror. The operator rests the pencil on the

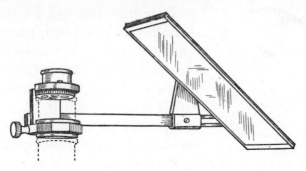

FIG. 22.—CAMERA LUCIDA

paper, then, when he looks through the microscope, he will see his hand, or at least the tip of
the pencil as well as the object. The pencil point
is then traced round the outline of the object or
whatever part he wishes to draw and in doing
this the pencil is marking the paper correspondingly at the side.

It is very difficult to get the hang of it and I
must confess that I have never been anything like
as successful with it as I would have wished.

I have been much more successful with a
cheaper and, in my experience, equally as successful a method. This method entails the use of a
glass disc (obtainable from any dealer in scientific instruments such as Bakers of Holborn), which
fits into the eye-piece—the lens is unscrewed and
the disc just dropped in; it will rest on the collar
within the eye-piece body.

241

R

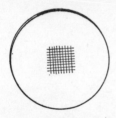

FIG. 23.—SQUARED
EYE-PIECE MICROMETER

Now, this disc will be ruled in half-millimetre squares and when the object on the stage is viewed it will be seen to have the network of magnified squares superimposed upon it. A sheet of squared paper should be at the side of the microscope and the next procedure depends on the size of the picture we wish to draw. For a picture of reasonable size it should be ruled off in centimetre squares, each square to correspond with the superimposed squares.

From then onwards the procedure is the same as that used in copying maps and this, as you may remember, consists in drawing from a squared map—one square at a time—on to squared paper. By this means the correct proportions are maintained and the outline will be reasonably accurate and can have the necessary refinements added after the disc has been removed from the eye-piece. The principal difficulty at first is to avoid mixing the squares up, but a little practice puts this to rights in no time.

CHAPTER XI

RINGING, FINISHING AND STORING

In this chapter the turntable indeed comes into its own. For all the operations are performed upon that instrument, that is to say, unless the operator is one of those very few people who can describe a circle free-hand. Without the turntable it is possible to make cement rings for fluid mounts and to add the finishing rings of cement and varnish; but the result is so clumsy looking (and, by the way, inefficient) that at all costs a turntable should either be made or purchased.

However, our cyclops (or whatever it is that we are concerned with) has been collected, killed and preserved. A mount, dry, wet or fluid, has been made and the final operation is that of rendering that mount as impervious as possible to outside influences. The slide has been cleaned, and where necessary, the mounting medium trimmed neatly to the edge of the cover-glass, and now it is necessary to run a film of cement around that edge so that part of it overlaps the top of the

cover and also the slide itself. As previously
advised use a good proprietary cement. Load
a camel or sable hair brush with the cement, set
the turntable spinning with a flick of the finger,
and, with the wrist steadied on the base gently
touch the edge of the cover-glass.

Most turntables are provided with two clips to
hold the slide, and the brass table has engraved
upon it circles corresponding to the standard

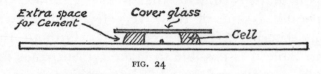

FIG. 24

cover-glass sizes; the slide should be so fixed
that the cover-glass corresponds exactly with its
respective circle, without any overlapping.

Our preliminary effort may not have completely 'ringed' the edge of the cover-glass, and so
a further coat will be necessary. For the sake of
neatness, as little as possible of the cement should
be used; just enough to touch the edge all round
at the same time touching the slide. A further
coat, when the first is dry, will be necessary with
both wet and fluid mounts. For further protec-
tion a coat of gold size may be applied and
finally, for effect alone, a coat of black. Some
mounters add to this with a thin ring of white and

another of red, but as we are more interested in microscope slides than musketry targets these can be omitted.

A useful tip in connexion with fluid mounts,

FIG. 25.—SLIDE CABINET

in particular, is to have the cover-glass a size larger than the cell itself. This gives additional cement space, consequently adding to the strength of the cell. (See Fig. 24).

As regards storing . slides mounted with Canada balsam are the only kind that can, with safety, be stored edgewise, all others must be stored flat.

Cardboard storing cabinets are quite inexpensive but, if one is adept with a fretsaw, cigarette tins can be utilized very well. Cavities, slightly

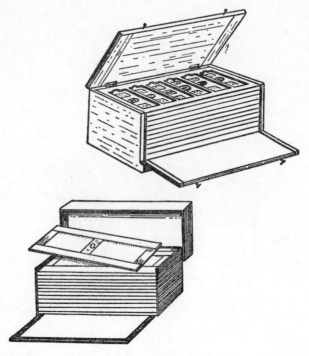

FIG. 26.—SLIDE CABINETS

larger than the size of the slides, can be cut in three-ply wood and a backing of cardboard affixed, the whole being so made as to fit comfortably in the tin. The small cabinet so made is useful for slipping in the pocket when taking your latest batch of slides to a friend's house.

Keep the cabinet, no matter how fine or how humble it may be, in a dry place and go over the collection from time to time to make sure that the cement is doing its work properly.

The following list should be of service to the beginner and, perhaps, to the advanced student as well. It is not intended to be comprehensive, by any means; neither, for that matter, does it necessarily include the best, or the only, sources from which materials can be obtained. The point is, they are all known to the author and can be recommended.

BAKER, C., OF HOLBORN, LTD., 244 High Holborn, London, W.C.1 : New and second-hand apparatus, specimen slides, accessories of all kinds; literature.

BOOTS THE CHEMISTS: All ordinary chemicals, others must be ordered specially.

BROADHURST, CLARKSON & CO. LTD., 63 Farringdon Road, London, E.C.1 : New and second-hand microscopes and accessories.

BRUNNINGS (HOLBORN) LTD., 135 High Holborn, London, W.C.1 : New and second-hand microscopes and accessories.

CLARKSON, A., & CO. LTD., 338 High Holborn, London, W.C.1 : New and second-hand apparatus; microscopes for hire.

FLATTERS & GARNETT LTD., 309 Oxford Road, Manchester 13 : Microscopes, accessories, mounted preparations and all chemicals.

GRIFFIN & GEORGE LTD., 285 Ealing Road, Alperton, Middlesex: Scientific instruments, laboratory equipment and all chemicals.

HAIG, L., Beam Brook, Newdigate, Surrey : Freshwater microscopic organisms.

MARINE BIOLOGICAL ASSOCIATION OF THE UNITED KINGDOM, Citadel Hill, Plymouth, Devon: Marine specimens, microscopic or otherwise, living or preserved; also nets, trawls, dredges and so forth.

WATKINS & DONCASTER, 110 Park View Road, Welling, Kent: Insects and insect collecting apparatus.

WATSON, W., & SONS, LTD., 313 High Holborn, London, W.C.1: Microscopes, accessories, mounted preparations and mounting media.

PERIODICAL

The Microscope, the British Journal of Microscopy and Photomicrography, 4 New Zealand Avenue, Barbican, London, E.C.1. Published every two months.

INDEX

INDEX

TEXT PRINTED IN GREAT BRITAIN BY EBENEZER BAYLIS AND SON, LTD.,
THE TRINITY PRESS, WORCESTER. AND LONDON
PLATES PRINTED IN GREAT BRITAIN BY
HENRY STONE AND SON, (PRINTERS) LTD., BANBURY
285 . 462